PINACOTECA

D0573456

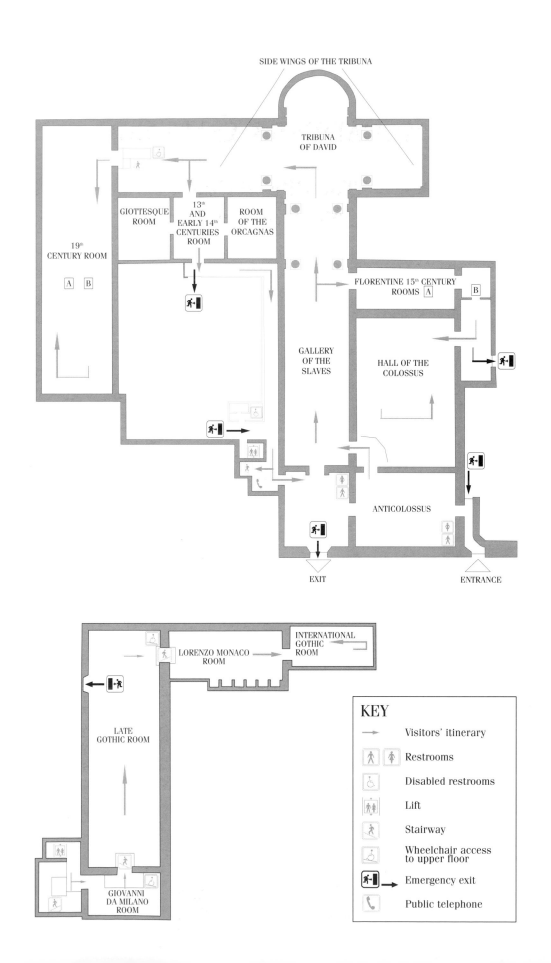

SIDE WINGS OF THE TRIBUNA

TRIBUNA OF DAVID

GIOTTESQUE ROOM

13th AND EARLY 14th CENTURIES ROOM

ROOM OF THE ORCAGNAS

19th CENTURY ROOM

A B

FLORENTINE 15th CENTURY ROOMS A

B

GALLERY OF THE SLAVES

HALL OF THE COLOSSUS

ANTICOLOSSUS

EXIT

ENTRANCE

INTERNATIONAL GOTHIC ROOM

LORENZO MONACO ROOM

LATE GOTHIC ROOM

GIOVANNI DA MILANO ROOM

KEY

→ Visitors' itinerary

Restrooms

Disabled restrooms

Lift

Stairway

Wheelchair access to upper floor

Emergency exit

Public telephone

ACCADEMIA GALLERY

The Official Guide
All of the Works

GIUNTI

FIRENZE
MVSEI

Texts
Franca Falletti, Marcella Anglani

Managing Editor
Claudio Pescio

Editor
Augusta Tosone

Translation
Ailsa Wood for Lexis, Florence and Catherine Frost

Graphics and page format
Rocío Isabel González

Photographs
Giunti Archive and Foto Rabatti-Domingie, Florence

This guide is a complete catalogue of all the works exhibited in the Gallery, room by room. For each room there is a plan showing the arrangement of the works of art. The encircled numbers refer to the lists in which all the works are catalogued. The small images appearing beside some numbers, in the border around the floor plan, indicate that a comment on these works appears on the following pages.

© 1999 Ministry of Artistic and Environmental Heritage –
Superintendence for Artistic and Historical Patrimony for the districts of Florence, Pistoia and Prato

No part of this publication may be reproduced in any form or by any means.

Editorial production of Giunti Gruppo Editoriale, Florence
Third edition: May 2001
ISBN 88-09-01344-1

Contents

Presentation

ENOUGH BOOKS HAVE been written about the public museums in Florence run by the Fine Arts and Historic Works Commission to fill a large library. This is hardly surprising when one considers that the artistic heritage preserved in our museums has been famous throughout the world for centuries. For hundreds of years writers, scholars and travellers of every nationality and country have been attempting to describe all that the Florentine museums contain. They have made great efforts to explain why these museums are so fascinating, and to lead a path through paintings and sculptures for both the uninformed but willing visitor and the refined and jaded intellectual.

Over time, however, the museums have altered their aspect and their layout, the exhibitions have been arranged in new ways, the collections have been enriched (or impoverished). Attributions of works in the museums have also changed, restorations have transformed the appearance of many pieces, the rise and fall of aesthetic tendencies have led to reorganisation and the exhibition of differing works. All these things are constantly taking place within the public collections because museology and the history of art, like any intellectual endeavour, are in a constant state of progress and transformation. This explains why the literature surrounding the Florentine museums (like that of any of the world's great art collections) is so immense, and in a process of continual updating and change.

The perfect, definitive guide to a museum, any museum, does not and cannot exist.

The premise seems obvious, but is nonetheless necessary in order to understand the point of the publication introduced by these lines. From the moment when, in accordance with the application of the Ronchey Law 4/93, the Giunti publishing house group took over the running of the support services within the Florentine museum system, it was decided to start at once on a standardised series of illustrated guides. These guides, displaying the cuneiform flower of "Firenze Musei" on the cover, guarantee that at the year of publication the state of each museum is exactly that described in the guide.

Certain things are obviously necessary if a museum guide is to aspire to reliability, official standing and at the same time enjoy a wide distribution: accuracy of information, high quality reproductions and – not least – a clearly written text (without, naturally, being banal or lacking in precision). Readers will judge for themselves if the guide which follows this introduction reaches these standards. I have no doubt that this will be a serious and committed judgement, just as myself and the Publisher of this guide have been serious and committed in attempting to meet the cultural needs of whoever visits our museums in the best way and with every possible care.

Head of the Fine Arts
and Historic Works Commission
of Florence, Pistoia and Prato
Antonio Paolucci

Introduction

THE ACCADEMIA GALLERY possesses and exhibits an amazing display of almost three hundred paintings covering a span of three centuries (Fourteenth, Fifteenth, and Sixteenth), a unique collection of 84 Russian Icons acquired by the Grand Dukes of Lorraine in the mid-Eighteenth century, and a grandiose Nineteenth century gallery of plaster casts including the original models of the major works of Lorenzo Bartolini and Luigi Pampaloni.

A new section now being prepared, that of musical instruments, will open to the public next year, displaying the unique historical collection of the Cherubini Conservatory, linked to the Gallery through special agreements. Obviously, the reasons for visiting this museum are many indeed.

Despite all this, everyone knows that the long, impatient lines of tourists who cross the threshold of the Accademia Gallery each day are really attracted almost exclusively by the myth of Michelangelo's David. *In 1998 there were over a million visitors, many of whom barely glanced at the painting collection and may not even have noticed the Nineteenth century Room. This phenomenon is rather recent, at least in its present frenzied form, and has aroused the curiosity of journalists and authors, historians, psychologists and sociologists. The magic power of the great white fetish is purposely enhanced by the architecture of the hall, which took the shape of a Latin cross when the Gallery of the* Slaves *was built leading up to De Fabris' Tribuna. Moreover, it must be admitted that this hero, already victorious before the fight, represents what modern man is seeking above all else: the reassuring certainty of pure, steadfast strength, a negation of the hesitancy and incertitude of life. And the* Slaves, *with their laborious struggle to emerge from the raw material, seem to have been placed here expressly to arouse an anxiety that the vision of the* David *immediately dispels.*

The heavy sense of the daily struggle to exceed the limitations of human nature is almost overpowering as we enter, but at the back of the great hall lit up by its skylight the world's most famous silhouette already towers above in its stance of classic repose: perfect, calm, in total equilibrium.

Far above any anxious struggle, untouched by defeat, David *exemplifies the secret desire of all.*

*The Director
of the Accademia Gallery
Franca Falletti*

History of the Gallery

a

b

The origins of the Accademia Gallery date back to 1784, when the Grand Duke of Tuscany Pietro Leopoldo brought together various art schools and organizations – such as the Accademia delle Arti del Disegno (Academy of Drawing), founded by Giorgio Vasari under the patronage of Cosimo I in 1563 – to form the new Accademia di Belle Arti (Academy of Fine Arts), a public art school.

Two buildings in particular were restructured to create the new Accademia: the Fourteenth century Hospital of San Matteo and the Convent of San Niccolò di Cafaggio. The two great hospital wards for men and for women were rebuilt as well-lit galleries designed to stimulate and instruct young people who had chosen art as a career, while providing them with models to copy. Plaster casts, drawings and models were placed in the former mens'

a. Moving Michelangelo's *David* from Piazza della Signoria to the Accademia di Belle Arti Gallery, *from "Nuova Illustrazione Universale", year I, no. 6, January 18, 1874, p. 48.*

b. Michelangelo's *David* during transport to the Accademia di Belle Arti, *Photographic Archives of the Superintendence for Artistic and Historical Patrimony of Florence.*

c. Odoardo Borrani, The Accademia Gallery in Florence (c. 1860), *oil on canvas, 25x38 cm, Galleria Nazionale d'Arte Moderna, Rome.*

d. Protection placed around the *David* during World War II.

e. Constructing protection around the *David* during World War II.

f. (p. 13) The Tribuna of *David* in the Accademia Gallery, post 1884-ante 1900, *Alinari Brothers photographic Archives, photo by Brogi.*

g. (p. 15) The Tribuna of *David*, post 1903-ante 1909, *Alinari Brothers photographic Archives, photo by Brogi.*

h. (p. 17) The Tribuna of *David*, post 1911-ante 1950, *Alinari Brothers photographic Archives, photo by Brogi.*

ward – adjacent to today's *Via Cesare Battisti,* on the premises of the Accademia di Belle Arti – while paintings were hung in the former womens' ward, now the Gallery's Nineteenth century Room.

It was for this educational purpose that the first core collection of today's Accademia Gallery was formed.

It included, in addition to two grandiose models by Giambologna – the Rape of the Sabine women and Virtue suppressing Vice – a number of plaster casts of classical statuary and a picture gallery consisting of the original collection of the Accademia del Disegno, which was continuously enriched by paintings transferred here from churches and monasteries suppressed by Pietro Leopoldo in 1786 and then by Napoleon in 1810.

Pietro Leopoldo also decided that works awarded prizes in the newly instituted acade-

mic competitions should be kept on permanent display. This gave rise, over the years, to a gallery presenting a broad sampling of the activity of teachers and pupils, testifying to the variety of artistic trends in Tuscany at the time. The importance of the new acquisitions is recorded in a description by Carlo Colzi in 1817. The Hall of Great Paintings, also known as the Galleria di Mezzogiorno (the present Nineteenth century) contained masterpieces such as the Santa Trinita Virgin by Cimabue, the Adoration of the Magi by Gentile da Fabriano, the Baptism of Christ by Verrocchio and Leonardo, and the Supper at Emmaus by Pontormo, all of which are now in the Uffizi, as well as works still in the Accademia Gallery today, including the decorative tiles from the Santa Croce Reliquary Cabinet by Taddeo Gaddi, the Annunciation by Lorenzo Monaco and the Deposition of Christ by Giovanni da

Milano. There were also a number of paintings by Beato Angelico, now in the San Marco Museum.

Not until 1841 was any improvement made in the highly confused arrangement of the paintings, when the President of the Accademia Antonio Ramirez of Montalvo decided to hang them in chronological order to illustrate the history of the Tuscan School from the Fourteenth to the Seventeenth centuries. The remaining Thirteenth and Fourteenth century paintings of unknown attribution or in poor state of conservation were left in the Antique Paintings Gallery (now the Hall of the Slaves) where they were so numerous as to entirely cover the walls. In 1817 there was also a "Prize-winning Works Room" containing eighteen works of art awarded first prize in the triennial painting and sculpture competitions. In 1821 this modern section was enlarged by the addition of prize-winning works from the annual Emulation and Pensionato competitions, all of which remained the property of the Accademia.

When Florence became capital of Italy at the time of the Unification, the city's museums, including the Accademia, underwent great changes. A new addition was the Modern Gallery, consisting of onehundredfortysix works transferred from Palazzo della Crocetta and arranged in six small rooms on the first floor of the Accademia that had previously belonged to the School of Declamation.

The Gallery thus became the first museum of modern art in the new State of Italy. From then on it was mentioned in all of the guidebooks as the Antique and Modern Gallery and increasingly recognized as an attraction for curious travellers as well a place for young artists to study innovations in Florentine art. Numerous requests were made to copy the paintings, the modern ones in particular, clearly demonstrating that the various collections still found a common denominator in the Gallery's educational mission.

In 1872 the museum structure was revolutionized when the Municipal Government decided to build a new room at the end of the Antique Paintings Gallery to house Michelangelo's David, which urgently needed to be moved from its unsheltered outdoor location in Piazza della Signoria. The architect assigned this task, Emilio De Fabris, designed an impressive Tribune which, placed scenographically at the end of the Antique Paintings Gallery and lighted from above by a skylight in the roof, was to welcome the David as the greatest of masterpieces. In early August 1873 the David, sliding on rails through the city streets, was transported to the Accademia where it was left enclosed in a wooden scaffolding for nine years while the Tribuna was being finished.

The arrival of the David and the project for building the Tribuna were crucial events for the fate of the Gallery. In 1875, on the occasion of the fourth centenary of Michelangelo's birth, the Accademia was deemed the most appropriate place to hold an exhibition of copies of the great artist's works. Exhibiting the plaster casts here would have found a valid rationale in the presence of the David, the reference point for the show, in a relationship of mutual enhancement. To create a space large enough for the exhibition it was requested that changes be made in the design of the Tribuna. No longer a square hall, it was to be shaped like a Greek cross. The right wing of the cross would then be extended to connect the Antique Paintings Gallery, then known as the Beato Angelico Gallery, to the parallel one of the Great Paintings, or of Perugino. The Michelangelo exhibition was by far the most important event in the centenary festivities held in Florence on September 13-16, 1875. For the occasion the Tribuna was draped with curtains to conceal the still-unfinished arches and vaults above the trabeation.

The wooden scaffolding was removed and the David, the only original statue in the show, became the fulcrum point of the entire exhibition, towering over all. This event had important museological consequences, giving decisive impetus to the creation of a Michelangelo Museum containing the plaster casts and photographs donated to the City of Florence. With farsighted intuition De Fabris wrote in 1877: "Should the Tribuna be completed, and the Michelangelo Museum inaugurated, it is certain that the proceeds from the sale of tickets would increase substantially, considering that while the importance of the gallery now is

only relative, it would then become so great that no foreigner would come to Florence without visiting it".

The architect Emilio De Fabris was the true artificer of the Michelangelo Museum, inaugurated on July 22, 1882. In the vestibule of the Tribuna, plaster casts of the Medici Tombs *were placed against the walls with the seated statues of* Lorenzo *and* Giuliano de' Medici *above them. At the back of the Tribuna's left wing, the shorter one, stood the Mo-ses. In the right wing were plaster casts of the artist's most famous works; at the center, under the tribunal arch, was a copy of the St. Peter's* Pietà, *while copies of the* Rondanini Pietà *and the* Minerva Christ *were placed at the corners of the piers.*

In that same 1882 management of the Accademia's Antique and Modern Gallery was transferred from the Fine Arts Institute to the Museums Bureau, causing the conservational, historical and documentary functions of the museum to prevail over the promotional program for contemporary art. In fact, as long as academic teaching methods had been based on the exercise of copying, the picture gallery had remained closely bound to the Accademia's painting School. When that method was abandoned as obsolete and inconsonant with the needs of contemporary art, the emancipation of the galleries from academic control became an urgent necessity.

The separation of the Antique and Modern Gallery from the art school was underlined by the opening of a new entrance in Via Ricasoli and by re-arrangement of the Michelangelo Museum.

The position of the Tribuna remained the same up to the early Twentieth century, while the Antique Paintings sector underwent major changes that marked the end of a trend of scientific and vaguely positivistic museum culture. Moreover, the concept of the museum as a structure dedicated exclusively to conservation was undergoing revision at this time, in relation to a new way of confronting works of art, now considered to be the subject of pure contemplation and "not a series of objects to be arranged in rows like insects by entomologists, but living things".

These new museum concepts was to influ-ence the program for rearranging the Florentine galleries carried out by Cosimo Ridolfi, the Director from 1890 to 1903. During this period the Accademia Gallery definitively lost its original characteristics, as profound changes were made. In the first place, the works of art in the Great Paintings Gallery urgently needed restoration, and this was favorable to a new arrangement. Wooden partitions were used to divide the room into three areas, separating the Fourteenth and Fifteenth century paintings from those of the Seventeenth century.

Three new rooms were also created (the former Byzantine Rooms the actually Thir-teenth and Early Fourteenth centuries Room, Room of the Orcagnas and their followers, Giottesque Room) along the left wing of the Tribuna, providing a more dignified and lu-minous setting for the paintings of Botticelli (to whom two of the rooms were dedicated), of Perugino and their pupils. Ridolfi made these changes to adapt the Accademia Gallery to the new aesthetic appreciation of the Flo-rentine Fifteenth Century School then being proclaimed mainly by British collectors living in Florence.

The rediscovery of Botticelli, which had begun with Pater's studies and been confir-med by the extensive monograph written by Herbert Horne during his years in Florence, was becoming a real cult in the early years of the Twentieth century, generating great public enthusiasm. A period of renewed popularity suddenly opened up for the Accademia Gal-lery, with its numerous Fifteenth century paintings. With the dignity and prominence conferred on them by their new arrangement, these paintings became a pole of attraction equal to or greater than that of the David *and Michelangelo's other works.*

Ridolfi then decided to put in "more appro-priate state" the hall leading to the Tribuna, where Thirteenth and Fourteenth century pa-nels and polyptychs were amassed in utter confusion. Radical changes were made in the arrangement of this hall. The paintings were removed and the walls adorned with rich tapestries depicting Stories of Adam and Eve. *Plaster casts of some of Michelangelo's minor works were placed along both side walls. The*

paintings that had been removed were then hung in the three rooms adjoining the Hall (now the Florentine Rooms), suitably decorated and lighted, the first of which was dedicated to Beato Angelico. This arrangement lasted only a few years since in 1919 works of capital importance to the Florentine School – Giotto and Cimabue's Majesty, Gentile da Fabriano's Adoration of the Magi, Masolino and Masaccio's Saint Anne Metterza, Botticelli's Primavera and many others were moved to the Uffizi Gallery, and in 1922 the conspicuous group of paintings by Beato Angelico went to establish the new San Marco Museum. Almost contemporaneously, in 1914, an agreement was stipulated between the State and the Municipality to group various collections of modern art in a single museum set up in 1920 on the second floor of Palazzo Pitti. The modern works of the Accademia Gallery, in part dispersed among various State and Municipal storage deposits, were transferred to their new home.

After having lost so many of its paintings the Gallery could no longer call itself the Antique and Modern Gallery. From now on it was to be Accademia Gallery or, for a few more years, Michelangelo Museum. The arrangement of the latter has also undergone numerous changes up to the present.

Controversy over the arrangement of the museum flared up again in the first decade of the Twentieth century, in relation to the question of placing a copy of the David in Piazza della Signoria. The presence of plaster casts in a public gallery, inserted within a context still linked to educational ideals and positivist/historical objectives, now seemed entirely unjustified. In line with the new aesthetic canons, authenticity became the guiding principle of the Gallery's Director Corrado Ricci, and most of the plaster casts kept here since the centenary exhibition were removed and replaced by original works of Michelangelo. At the same time, national newspapers were calling attention to the poor state of the Slaves in Buontalenti's Grotto in the Boboli Gardens, and to the St. Matthew "drowsing under the atrium of the Accademia". The Slaves were removed from Boboli, replaced by copies, and transferred to the Accademia Gallery in 1909.

That same year the School of Accademia delle Belle Arti, which had already contributed the model of the Fiume Torso in 1906, donated the St. Matthew. This group of works was further enriched by the Victory, transferred from the Bargello Museum in 1905. The plaster casts from the centenary exhibition, arranged by Ridolfi along the walls hung with tapestries, were replaced by the originals of the Slaves, the St. Matthew and the Victory, along with two plaster casts of the Louvre Slaves, while the model of the Fiume Torso was placed under the right arch of the Tribuna. The plaster casts of the Tombs, the Moses, the Rondanini Pietà, the Minerva Christ and the Vatican Pietà remained in their original places. In Ricci's arrangement based on the principle of authenticity, even these last plaster casts soon appeared inappropriate. However, it was only in 1938 that the casts of the two Pietà, the Moses, the Minerva Christ and the Tombs were definitively moved to the Plaster Casts Collection of the Porta Romana Art School. The casts of the Slaves were the last to leave the Accademia in 1946, transferred to the Casa Buonarroti Museum where in 1950 a ground-floor room was arranged to exhibit copies of some of Michelangelo's works.

The collection of the originals also underwent changes before taking on its present-day aspect. In 1921, with the closure of the Dante Year and the celebration of victory in World War I, Ugo Ojetti suggested that, for the occasion, the Victory should be brought back to the Hall of the Five Hundred in Palazzo Vecchio. In 1939 the State of Italy purchased for the Accademia the Palestrina Pietà, coming from a chapel in Palazzo Barberini at Palestrina, the authenticity of which is now denied by the most authoritative scholars. Lastly, in 1965, the Fiume Torso was requested by Charles Tolnay, to join the other models in the Casa Buonarroti.

In the 1930s the Hall of the Colossus and that of the Anticolossus were annexed to the Gallery. These large rooms provided a perfect setting for the great altarpieces of the Florentine Sixteenth century masters such as Massimo Albertinelli, Bronzino, Alessandro Allori, Santi di Tito, and Passignano.

After the war, during rearrangement of the

Uffizi Gallery, some large paintings were moved to the Accademia, including the Sixteenth century Assumption *by Perugino and* Deposition *by Perugino and Filippino Lippi.*

In the 1950s, under the direction of Luisa Becherucci, the Hall of the Colossus, illustrating the course of art in the Fifteenth and Sixteenth centuries, was organized on a more historical basis, as can be seen in the works of Perugino, Fra Bartolomeo, Granacci, Bugiardini and Sogliani. In the Hall of the Anticolossus, now occupied by the bookshop and ticket office, were placed some works coming from the Uffizi, including the Young St. John *from the school of Raphael and the* Venus and Cupid *by Pontormo. These works, in addition to those of Bronzino and Allori already present, clearly illustrated the development of the "modern manner" in the Sixteenth century. Only in the 1980s was this arrangement dismantled and the paintings hung in the Tribuna in place of the tapestries, to underline their direct and indirect relationship with the work of Michelangelo.*

Subsequent Directors have opposed the tendency – which had emerged in the post-World War I period – to proceed without a specific direction or long-term project. From direction of Luciano Bellosi, through the important years of Giorgio Bonsanti, up to the current Director Franca Falletti, a continuous attempt has been made to trace a guiding principle on which to construct the identity of the Accademia Gallery.

This project took concrete shape in the years between 1983 and 1985 with the arrangement of the Nineteenth century Room and that of the Late Fourteenth century Room on the first floor, supervised by Angelo Tartuferi in 1998. The opening to the public of the latter rooms confirmed the museum's chronological, stylistic and historical direction, providing a continuous panorama, albeit in different groups of rooms, of Florentine art from the late Thirteenth to the late Sixteenth centuries, in accordance with the original principles of the Accademia as conceived by Pietro Leopoldo. What now re-emerges in all its significance is the value of the Accademia as school of instruction and exemplification of the highest artistic manifestations in three centuries of history. *Within this context, the Collection of Russian Icons on the first floor also testifies to the precious heritage of the Lorraine family.*

The Nineteenth century Room, with the plaster casts by Bartolini and Pampaloni and the paintings, few but significant, by pupils and professors of the Accademia di Belle Arti, unites the Accademia to the Gallery, rebuilding a bridge of historical significance and recalling how Accademia and Gallery were once joined in a common project to produce and nourish art.

As the origins of the Gallery have been retrieved, links with the adjoining Cherubini Conservatory and Opificio delle Pietre Dure have inevitably been restored. All of these institutions, in fact, grew out of a unified project, perhaps the most culturally significant initiative of the Lorraine government, that of constructing, in the block between today's Via Ricasoli, Via degli Alfani, Via dei Servi and Via Cesare Battisti, a true citadel of the arts. This is the basis for the current Director's project for opening to the public a Museum of Musical Instruments, consisting of the historical collection of the Cherubini Conservatory, which will be under the same management as the Accademia Gallery. And it is possible that in the near future the itinerary may be completed by coordinated access to the Museum of the Opificio delle Pietre Dure, next door to the Cherubini Conservatory.

Marcella Anglani

The Collection of Musical Instruments

Four large rooms in the adjoining Luigi Cherubini Conservatory (the State School of Music) are currently being prepared in the Accademia Gallery to accommodate the Historical Collection of Musical Instruments.

The Collection will include items unique in the world, like the so-called Medici viola, made in 1690 by Antonio Stradivari to the commission of Prince Ferdinando de' Medici, or the psaltery made in three types of marble, decorated with the Medici coat of arms and a rhyming dedication. The most important group in the exhibition comes from the collection of the Grand Dukes, first the Medici and later the Lorraines, and was brought from Palazzo Pitti in 1863 and 1926.

The Museum of musical instruments will be linked to the Accademia Gallery and will become a part of its display route, in keeping with the spirit of historical conservation which has also been the basis for other important preparatory additions in recent years, like the Nineteenth century Room. The Music School was originally part of the Accademia di Belle Arti, and was the second class after that which included painting, sculpture and architecture, and before applied arts.

a

b

c

a. Tenor viola by Antonio Stradivari (1690), known as *Medici viola*.

b. Vertical piano by Domenico del Mela.

c. Marble psaltery from the Medici's collection.

Gallery of the Slaves

The present-day Gallery of the Slaves *occupies the area once called the Gallery of Antique Paintings in which, starting from 1817, a great number of Thirteenth and Fourteenth century panel paintings and polyptychs, of unknown attribution and poor state of conservation, were kept. With the arrival of the* David *and the creation of the Michelangelo Museum the arrangement of the Gallery was radically changed; between the Nineteenth and Twentieth century the hall was dismantled, the Medieval paintings removed, the walls decorated with tapestries and the area dedicated to exhibiting plaster casts of Michelangelo's minor works. In 1909 the* Slaves *were moved from Buontalenti's Grotto in the Boboli Gardens to the Accademia Gallery, and this hall gradually became a unique collection of the great sculptor's original works. Today the arrangements of the* Slaves, *along the sides of the Gallery, seems purposely designed to lead the visitor, in a growing crescendo of emotion, to the feet of Michelangelo's colossus.*

The works

1. DANIELE DA VOLTERRA
Bust of Michelangelo
c. 1566
Bronze; height 59 cm
Sculptures Inv. no. 1083

2. MICHELANGELO BUONARROTI
Slaves: The Young Slave
c. 1530
Marble; height 256 cm
Sculptures Inv. no. 1079

3. MICHELANGELO BUONARROTI
Slaves: The Awakening Slave
c. 1530
Marble; height 267 cm
Sculptures Inv. no. 1078

4. MICHELANGELO BUONARROTI
Slaves: Atlas
c. 1530
Marble; height 277 cm
Sculptures Inv. no. 1080

5. MICHELANGELO BUONARROTI
St. Matthew
1505-1506
Marble; height 271 cm
Sculptures Inv. no. 1077

6. MICHELANGELO BUONARROTI
Slaves: The Bearded Slave
c. 1530
Marble; height 263 cm
Sculptures Inv. no. 1081

7. MICHELANGELO BUONARROTI
(ATTRIBUTED TO)
Pietà from Palestrina
(Pietà with St. John the Evangelist)
c. 1547-1559
Marble; height 251 cm
Sculptures Inv. no. 1319

MICHELANGELO'S *SLAVES*

The four sculptures – exhibited in this room along with other works by Michelangelo and by artists influenced by him – were intended to decorate the base of a complicated mausoleum to be raised in the basilica of St. Peter's in the Vatican as the tomb of Pope Julius II della Rovere. The project had a tormented history and after undergoing radical modifications to reduce the size, the mausoleum was placed in San Pietro in Vincoli where it remains to this day.
The four unfinished Slaves *not used on the tomb were donated after Michelangelo's death to Grand Duke Cosimo I de' Medici and placed by him in the Buontalenti Grotto in Boboli, from where they were transferred to the Accademia in 1909.*
The Slaves *are a good introduction to an understanding of Michelangelo's unfinished work. Their forms, not brought to a state of perfection, manage to confer a universal meaning on that sensation of an immense struggle to free themselves from the marble vividly perceived by all who view them.*

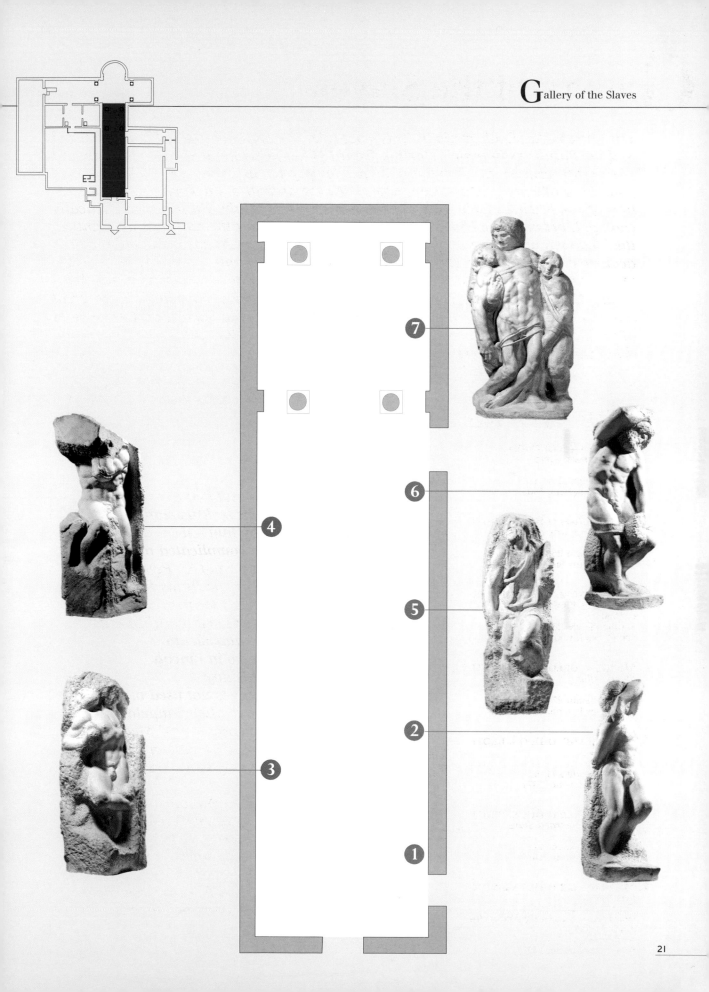

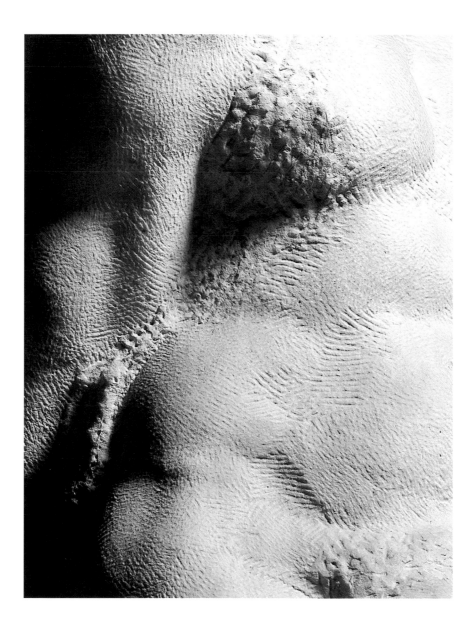

2

MICHELANGELO BUONARROTI
Slaves:
The Young Slave

The first of the four *Slaves* displayed along the walls of the Gallery leading to the Tribuna of *David* is known as *The Young Slave*. He is depicted with slightly bent knees, as if burdened by a weary step, and his left arm is folded across his face, while his right arm slips behind his hip. Emerging from a block of marble which, at the back, seems still untouched, the different parts of the figure itself have been finished to various degrees: the head is roughly outlined, the left side of the torso more finished than the right. However on each part of the surface the marks of the tools used by Michelangelo in his long creative process are still visible.

3

MICHELANGELO BUONARROTI
Slaves:
The Awakening Slave

The powerful limbs of this virile figure struggle to emerge from one side of the imposing block of marble.

The roughly outlined features of the face can barely be made out, and the right leg, bent over the left, protrudes forward to mirror the movement of the right arm.
The result is a tense and dynamic composition which fully expresses the struggle of the material to break out of its own limits.

25

4

MICHELANGELO BUONARROTI
Slaves: Atlas

This *Slave* is known as *Atlas* because he seems to be carrying a huge weight on his head; however the weight is in fact the head itself, which is not separate and cannot be distinguished. The legs seem to be parted and the bent arms struggle to support the massive weight bearing down on the wide shoulders. *Atlas*, perhaps more than the other *Slaves*, seems to express energy struggling to emerge from the marble.

5

MICHELANGELO BUONARROTI
St. Matthew

The *St. Matthew* was originally to be part of a series of the twelve apostles, a commission given to Michelangelo in 1503 for the columns of Florence Cathedral. In the event the sculptor only worked on one, which is also unfinished, for which reason it was left abandoned in the Opera del Duono (Cathedral Vestry Board) courtyard until 1831. It was moved to the Accademia di Belle Arti where it was first placed in a niche in the courtyard and later, in 1909, in the Gallery near the *Slaves*.

6

MICHELANGELO BUONARROTI
Slaves:
The Bearded Slave

The Bearded Slave is the most nearly finished of the four *Slaves* by Michelangelo .
The face is covered by a thick, curly beard and the thighs are encircled by a strip of cloth. The fine modelling of the torso, the surface finished with soft sensitivity to light and clear evidence of relief modelling, reveals a careful and profound study of anatomy.
The sculpture is traversed below the hips by a fracture, the origin of which is unknown.

7

MICHELANGELO BUONARROTI
(ATTRIBUITED TO)
Pietà from Palestrina

Among the large sculptures attributed to Michelangelo, the *Pietà from Palestrina* (c. 1547-1559) is the only one not recorded in the sources or in any document in the archives. It has been in the Accademia since 1939, purchased by the State of Italy from a chapel in Palazzo Barberini at Palestrina.

It was mentioned for the first time as a "rough draft" by Michelangelo in a historical publication on Palestrina dated 1736. The lack of certain documentation led to a lengthy discussion on its attribution, involving numerous experts, after the presentation of the work in modern times (Garnier 1907). Many art historians, noting the presence of disproportion, unusual softness of the forms and a certain flatness, have attributed this work to one of the Maestro's followers.

Tribuna of David

Between 1872 and 1882 the architect Emilio De Fabris designed, in the Accademia Gallery, a hall in the shape of a Latin cross at the center of which, under a circular skylight, the David *would be placed. In early August of 1873 the* David, *sliding on rails through the streets of Florence, was moved to the Accademia. Only in 1882 was work on the Tribuna and the two side wings completed.*

At first copies of Michelangelo's works were exhibited in the side wings. In the early Twentieth century the Michelangelo Museum was dismantled and the walls were decorated with tapestries. It was only in the 1980s that the tapestries were replaced by large paintings by Sixteenth century artists, to emphasize their relationship with Michelangelo's work.

The works

1. MICHELANGELO BUONARROTI
David
1501-1504
Marble
height 517 cm
Sculptures Inv. no. 1076

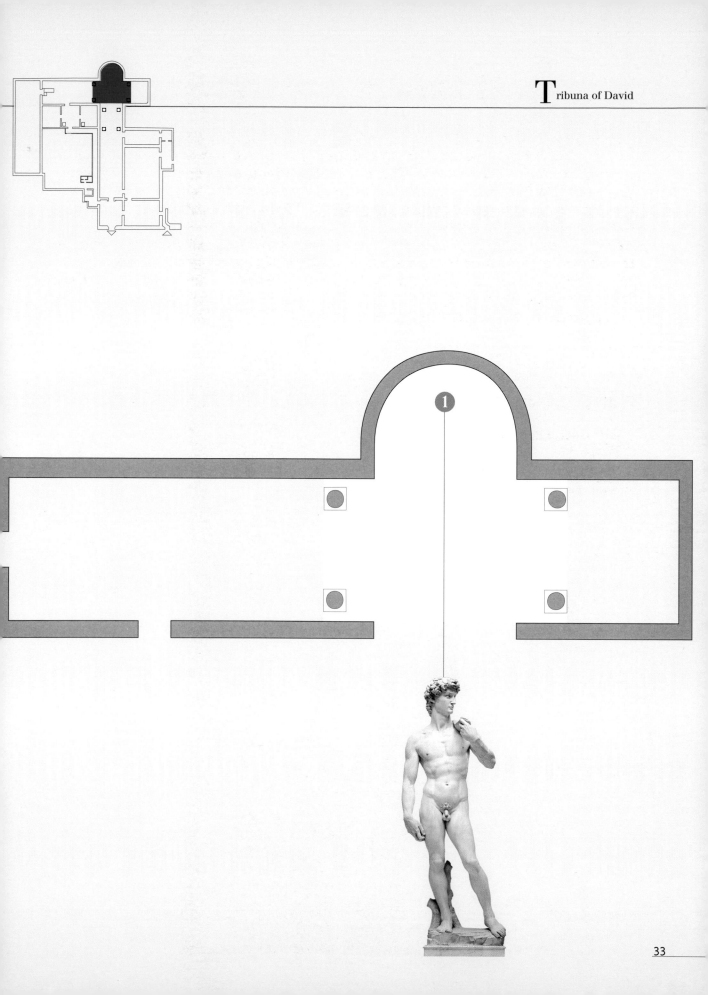

1

1

MICHELANGELO BUONARROTI
David

The *David* was originally commissioned by the Florence Opera del Duomo to be placed as a decoration in the Cathedral. It was sculpted by Michelangelo between 1501 and 1504, when it was placed in front of Palazzo Vecchio, following much discussion and debate among the main contemporary Florentine artists. The Giant, as it became known, became a symbol of the civil freedom and virtue of republican Florence, and it remained in its original location until 1873 when it was transferred, using a com-

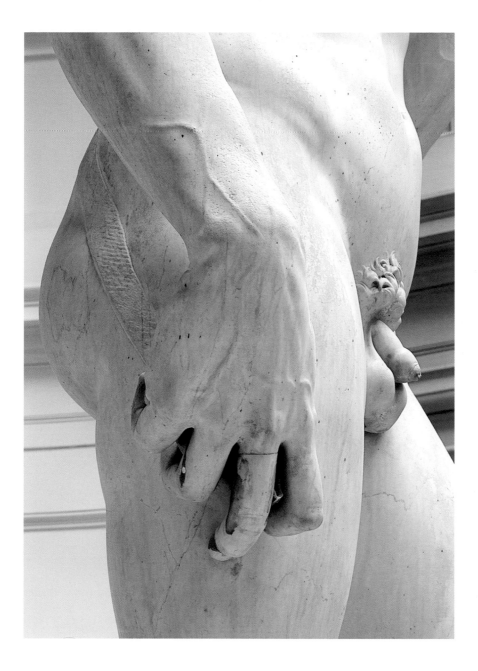

plex support structure resting on wheels, inside the Accademia di Belle Arti, where it can still be admired today.

The sculpture portrays the future king of Israel in a similar form and pose to a triumphant hero of classical Greece. This clearly distances Michelangelo's *David* from those previously made by Donatello and Verrocchio which, adhering more closely to the biblical text, depicted David as a slender boy, unaware of his divine mission.

The statue's perfect modelling, the calm and determined strength of the expression and its imposing size have made it one of the best-known and most admired works of art in the world.

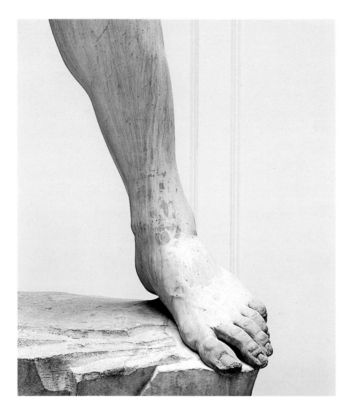

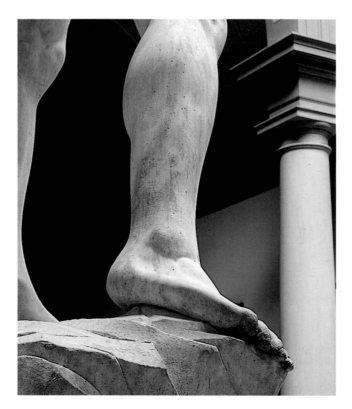

Florentine Fifteenth Century Rooms: A

These rooms are dedicated to Fifteenth century paintings. While some masterpieces are displayed here, like the canvas showing Scenes of Hermit life *by Paolo Uccello and the* Virgin and Child with the infant St. John and two Angels *by Botticelli, the everyday production of the most active studios in Renaissance Florence is also represented.*

Among these were Ghirlandaio's and Cosimo Rosselli's, where the great masters worked in close contact with assistants and errand boys on the numerous paintings which were to decorate the thousands altars the city's churches, large and small.

The works

1. MARIOTTO DI CRISTOFANO
The marriage of St. Catherine
In the back: *Resurrection of Christ*
c. 1445
Tempera on wood
160x152 cm (each)
Inv. 1890 nos. 3162, 3164

2. PAOLO UCCELLO (below)
Scenes of Hermit life or *Thebaid*
c. 1460
Tempera on canvas
81x111 cm
Inv. 1890 no. 5381

3. NERI DI BICCI (above)
Saints
c. 1444-1453
Tempera on wood
130x89 cm
Inv. 1890 no. 3470

4. ANONYMOUS FLORENTINE
Holy Trinity and Saints
In the predella: *Annunciation*
c. 1470-1480
Tempera on wood
220x134 cm
Inv. 1890 no. 3465

5. DOMENICO DI MICHELINO
Holy Trinity
In the predella: *Stories of Archangels*
c. 1460-1470
Tempera on wood
137x71.5 cm
Inv. 1890 no. 8636

6. MASTER OF THE JOHNSON NATIVITY AND FILIPPINO LIPPI
(below)
Annunciation
c. 1460-1470
Tempera on wood
184x190 cm
Inv. 1890 no. 4632

7. NERI DI BICCI (above)
Annunciation
c. 1464
Tempera on wood
178x170 cm
Inv. 1890 no. 8622

8. BENOZZO GOZZOLI
St. Bartholomew, St. John the Baptist, St. James the Elder
c. 1462
Tempera on wood
171x22.5 cm
Inv. 1890 no. 8620

DOMENICO DI MICHELINO
The Archangel Michael with St. Lawrence and St. Leonard
c. 1469
Tempera on wood
171x22.5 cm
Inv. 1890 no. 8621

9. COSIMO ROSSELLI (below)
St. Barbara between St. John the Baptist and St. Matthew
c. 1470
Tempera on wood
207x204 cm
Inv. 1890 no. 8635

10. DOMENICO DI MICHELINO
(above)
The three Archangels and Tobiolo
c. 1460-1470
Tempera on wood
183x180 cm
Inv. 1890 no. 8624

11. COSIMO ROSSELLI (below)
Noah and king David
Moses and Abraham
c. 1460
Tempera on wood
20.5x57 cm (each)
Inv. 1890 nos. 8632, 8633

12. PSEUDO PIER FRANCESCO FLORENTINE (above)
The Virgin in adoration of the Child
After 1459
Tempera on wood
79x55.5 cm
Inv. 1890 no. 3158

13. MASTER OF THE CASTELLO NATIVITY
Nativity
In the predella: *Four Prophets*
c. 1460
Tempera on wood
213x98 cm
Dep. inv. no. 171

14. LO SCHEGGIA (below)
Wedding procession
or *Cassone (Chest) Adimari*
c. 1450
Tempera on wood
63x280 cm
Inv. 1890 no. 8457

15. ALESSO BALDOVINETTI (above)
Holy Trinity and St. Benedict and St. Giovanni Gualberto
c. 1472
Tempera on wood
238x284 cm
Inv. 1890 no. 8637

16. GIOVAN FRANCESCO DA RIMINI
St. Vincenzo Ferreri
In the predella:
Three scenes from the life of the Saint
mid-XV century
Tempera on wood
145x70 cm
Inv. 1890 no. 3461

17. ANDREA DI GIUSTO
Virgin with Child and two Angels
First half of the XV century
Tempera on wood
117x57 cm
Inv. 1890 no. 3160

18. ANDREA DI GIUSTO (below)
Madonna of the Girdle and Saints
In the predella:
Martyrdom of St. Catherine, Death of the Virgin
and *Stigmata of St. Francis*
1437
Tempera on wood
185x220 cm
Inv. 1890 no. 3236

19. DOMENICO DI MICHELINO AND STUDIO (above)
Virgin with Child and Saints
c. 1460-1470
Tempera on wood
178x186 cm
Inv. 1890 no. 3450

20. ANDREA DI GIUSTO
Virgin with Child, two Angels and Christ as the Man of Sorrows
First decades of the XV century
Tempera on wood
101x49 cm
Inv. 1890 no. 6004

21. MARIOTTO DI CRISTOFANO
Scenes from the Lives of Christ and of the Virgin
In the cuspids: *Annunciation* and *Assumption of the Virgin*
c. 1450-1457
Tempera on wood
225x175 cm
Inv. 1890 no. 8508

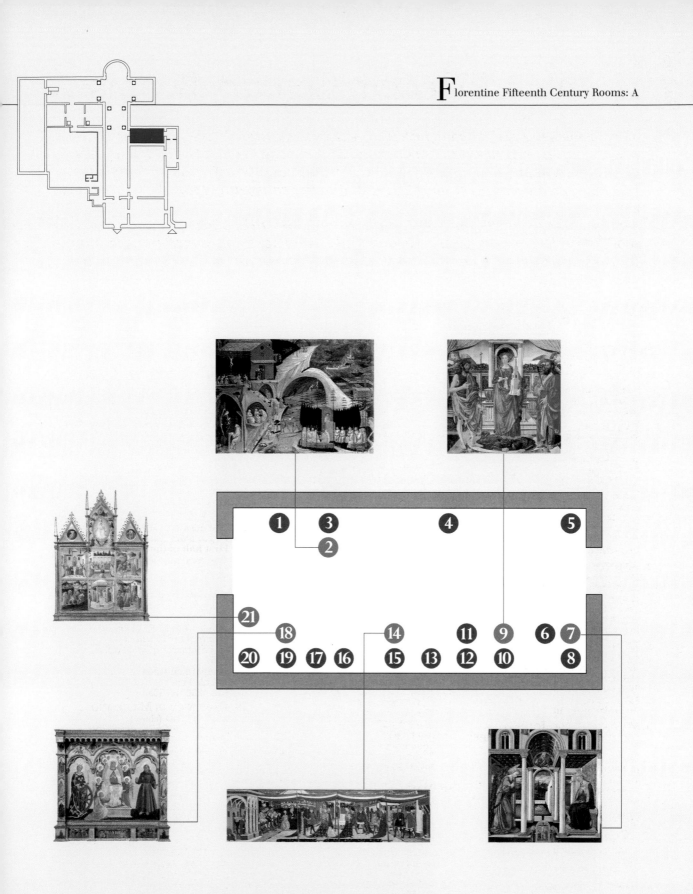

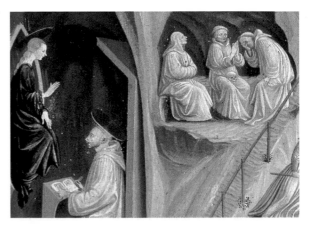

2

PAOLO UCCELLO
Scenes of Hermit life or *Thebaid*

The subject of this painting by Paolo Uccello is not easily interpreted but is certainly linked to a path of meditation and spiritual improvement through prayer. The following episodes can be identified: *The stigmata of St. Francis, St. Jerome worships the Crucifix, The appearance of the Virgin to St. Bernard* and *St. Benedict preaches to his brethren.*

7

NERI DI BICCI
Annunciation

This panel comes from the Church of Santa Maria del Sepolcro, known as "delle Campora", for which it was commissioned in 1464 by Agnolo Vettori, an outstanding figure in Fifteenth century Florentine politics, several times prior and gonfalonier of the Republic in 1458. Heir to an ancient Florentine studio, founded by his grandfather Lorenzo di Bicci and continued by his father, Bicci di Lorenzo, Neri di Bicci often re-produced traditional compositions over the years with his impeccable technique, making only the slightest modifications.

Worthy of note in this *Annunciation* (one of many painted by this artist) is the detail of the small board at the bottom showing the *Crucifixion*, and the complex architecture where the deep perspective leads the gaze to the landscape in the background.

43

9

COSIMO ROSSELLI
St. Barbara between
St. John the Baptist and St. Matthew

Cosimo Rosselli, head of a well-equipped, active family-run studio, painted this gorgeous panel for the Chapel of St. Barbara and St. Quiricus in the Basilica of Santissima Annunziata in Florence. This chapel belonged to the so-called "Teutonic Nation", i.e. to the Germans and Flemings. St. Barbara was the patron saint of artillery and therefore she is holding up the tower as a symbol of a line of fortification and crushing a conquered warrior beneath her feet. The composition of the painting (c. 1470) recalls details from works by other contemporary Florentine artists, like Pollaiuolo's panel for the Portuguese cardinal's Chapel in San Miniato and Ghirlandaio's fresco in the Church of Sant'Andrea in Cercina, and it is painted with skill and dignity.

14

LO SCHEGGIA
Wedding procession
or *Cassone (Chest) Adimari*

This was originally listed as *Cassone Adimari* because it was thought to be the front panel of a wedding chest belonging to the Adimari family. The painting (c. 1450) was later recognised as part of a "spalliera", a wall decoration, and was attributed to Giovanni di Ser Giovanni, known as Lo Scheggia, the brother of Masaccio. The images depicted here concern a wedding feast and portray the streets, monuments (the Baptistry can be seen on the left), landscapes and customs of Renaissance Florence with vivacity and extraordinary wealth of detail.

18

ANDREA DI GIUSTO
Madonna of the Girdle and Saints

This painting, dated 1437 and signed "Andrea de Florentia", comes from the Church of Santa Margherita in Cortona, and is the work of a painter active during the first half of the 15ᵗʰ century. The artist is clearly familiar with the great "modern" painters, such as Paolo Uccello and Beato Angelico, but solidly linked to the Gothic tradition, as this altarpiece shows in its use of gold-leaf background and the division of the space into three, which recalls the 14ᵗʰ century polyptychs.

21

MARIOTTO DI CRISTOFANO
*Scenes from the Lives
of Christ and of the Virgin*

This painting, dated from 1450-1457, coming from the Church of Sant'Andrea a Doccia, is made up of six panels portraying *Scenes from Christ' childhood*, the *Death of the Virgin*, and in the large central cusp, the *Assumption*.
The polyptych was attributed in the Nineteenth century to the school of Beato Angelico and subsequently to an artist influenced by Bicci di Lorenzo. In the 1960s it was noticed that similarities existed between this painting and the dual-face panel, present in the same room, representing the *Mystic marriage of St. Catherine* and the *Resurrection of Christ*, painted in 1445 by Mariotto di Cristofano, an artist whose style shows the influence of Beato Angelico and Masolino.

Florentine Fifteenth Century Rooms: B

The works

1. **FRANCESCO BOTTICINI**
St. Andrew in adoration of the Cross
1475-1499
Tempera on wood
63x43 cm
Inv. 1890 no. 8656

2. **JACOPO DEL SELLAIO** (below)
Christ deposed in the Sepulchre
1480-1490
Tempera on wood
38x42.5 cm
Inv. 1890 no. 8655

3. **PIETRO PERUGINO (?)** (above)
The Visitation
c. 1472-1473
Tempera on wood
32x34 cm
Inv. 1890 no. 8654

4. **DOMENICO GHIRLANDAIO**
St. Stephen between St. James and St. Peter
1493
Oil on wood
175x174 cm
Inv. 1890 no. 1621

5. **SEBASTIANO MAINARDI** (below)
Christ as the Man of Sorrows between the Virgin and St. John the Evangelist
1475-1500
Tempera on wood
97x71 cm
Inv. 1890 no. 8623

6. **BIAGIO D'ANTONIO** (above)
Announcing Angel, Eternal Father and *Our Lady of the Annunciation*
c. 1475
Tempera on wood
37x119 cm
Inv. 1890 no. 8619

7. **ANONYMOUS FLORENTINE** (below)
Martyrdom of St. Lawrence
c. 1480
Tempera on wood
54x38 cm
Inv. 1890 no. 6186

8. **ANONYMOUS FLORENTINE** (above)
Annunciation
c. 1490
Tempera on wood
13x50 cm
Inv. 1890 no. 8639

9. **ANONYMOUS FLORENTINE**
Eternal Father
c. 1500-1510
Tempera on wood
67x134 cm
Inv. 1890 no. 8631

10. **COSIMO ROSSELLI, STUDIO OF**
Enthroned Virgin (The Virgin of the Star)
c. 1470-1490
Tempera on wood
186x137 cm
Inv. 1890 no. 3205

11. **SANDRO BOTTICELLI**
Virgin with Child with the infant St. John and two Angels
c. 1468
Tempera on wood
85x64 cm
Inv. 1890 no. 3166

12. **SANDRO BOTTICELLI AND ASSISTANTS**
Virgin with Child and Saints
1480-1500
Tempera on canvas
177x205 cm
Inv. 1890 no. 4344

13. **SANDRO BOTTICELLI (?)**
Virgin of the Sea
c. 1475-1480
Oil on wood
40x28 cm
Inv. 1890 no. 8456

14. **FILIPPINO LIPPI**
St. John the Baptist
St. Mary Magdalene
c. 1496
Oil on wood
136x56 cm (each)
Inv. 1890 nos. 8653, 8651

15. **BARTOLOMEO DI GIOVANNI**
St. Francis receiving the stigmata
Deposition
St. Girolamo
c. 1500-1510
Tempera on wood
28x54 cm (each)
Inv. 1890 nos. 8629, 8628, 8627

16. **RAFFAELLINO DEL GARBO**
Christ rising from the Sepulchre
c. 1500-1505
Oil on wood
177x187 cm
Inv. 1890 no. 8363

17. **JACOPO DEL SELLAIO**
Deposition and Saints
c. 1491-1494
Tempera on wood
169x173 cm
Inv. 1890 no. 5069

18. **LORENZO DI CREDI**
Adoration of the Child
c. 1496-1500
Tempera on wood
137x143.5 cm
Inv. 1890 no. 8661

19. **GHERARDO DI GIOVANNI**
Virgin and Child with four Saints
c. 1480-1495
Tempera on wood
194x177 cm
Inv. 1890 no. 9149

20. **MASTER OF THE FIESOLE EPIPHANY**
Coronation of Maria
c. 1470-1475
Tempera on wood
154x92 cm
Inv. 1890 no. 490

21. **GHERARDO DI GIOVANNI**
Virgin in adoration of the Child with the infant St. John
1475-1480
Tempera on wood
112x60 cm
Inv. 1890 no. 8634

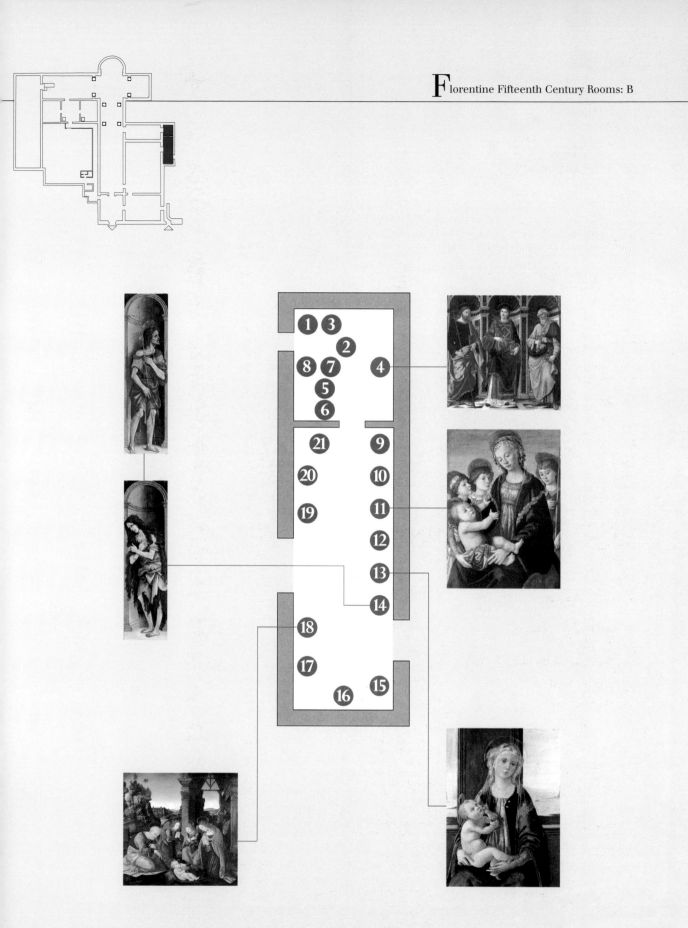

4

DOMENICO GHIRLANDAIO
St. Stephen between
St. James and St. Peter

In the past this panel was attributed to Sebastiano Mainardi, a pupil of Ghirlandaio, but it was recently recognised as work of the master himself. A few years after it was painted, perhaps in 1513, the figure of St. Stephen was repainted to look like St. Jerome, by the hand of Fra Bartolomeo, according to traditional accounts. Nineteenth century restoration work then cancelled this modification. In this composition the touch of Ghirlandaio, noted for his lively narrative and decorative elements, is conspicuous in the unusual majesty of the three sculptural figures which strikingly emerge from the "chiaroscuro" effect of the niches.

11

SANDRO BOTTICELLI
Virgin with Child with the infant St. John and two Angels

This work, from Botticelli's early phase, the clearly shows the stylistic characteristics of Filippo Lippi, in whose studio Sandro was still training. This composition with its diffuse structure was to be very successful in later years and was repeated in numerous terracotta bas-reliefs for private devotional use.

13

SANDRO BOTTICELLI (?)
Virgin of the Sea

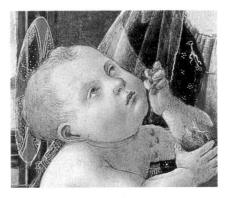

This small panel (c. 1475-1480), which owes its name to the dim seascape in the background, has always been one of the most admired works by visitors to the Gallery.

However the critics are still not in agreement over the attribution, vacillating between Botticelli and Filippino Lippi.

14

FILIPPINO LIPPI
St. John the Baptist
St. Mary Magdalene

These two paintings (c. 1496) were the side panels of an altarpiece having at the center a *Crucifixion with the Virgin and St. Francis* with gold-leaf background, originally placed in the Chapel of Francesco Valori in San Procolo.

The panels were divided in the mid-Eighteenth century and the central one was destroyed in Berlin in 1945 during World War II.

The two figures in the side panels, St. John the Baptist, consumed by repentance in the desert, and St. Mary Magdalene, are marked by the suffering of spiritual torment, emphasized by their emaciated appearance, tangled hair, torn clothing and bare feet.

In these figures Filippino revived the figurative tradition of the early Fifteenth century, especially as exemplified in polychrome wooden sculptures, to suggest the devout objective of art according to the dictates of the client Valori, one of Girolamo Savonarola's most important followers.

18

LORENZO DI CREDI
Adoration of the Child

The original location of this painting by Loren- zo di Credi is uncertain, some experts believ- ing it to come from the Convento dell'Annunzia- ta, others from the Convento delle Murate. Painted slightly later than the better known *Adoration* in the Uffizi (c. 1480-1485), it dates to the last decade in the Fifteenth century, a period in which Renaissance style was under- going dissolution.

Lorenzo di Credi assimilated Leonardo's innovations (both were pupils of Verrocchio) up to the point where they represented a break with the past. In this painting the symmetrical scheme, the view scaled plane by plane, and the sentimental effects of the figures testify to Lorenzo's rejection of Leonardo's perspective studies as well as his links to Fifteenth century tradition. In the landscape in the background and the small figures of shepherds at the left, the quality of the painting is reminiscent of Piero di Cosimo.

Hall of the Colossus

The name of this room is not, as is usually believed, taken from Giambologna's plaster model, now placed at its centre, but from the model of one of Montecavallo's Dioscuri, displayed here in the last century. The panels on display follow on in chronological order from the route of the Florentine rooms and are therefore by painters working in the early decades of the Sixteenth century.
The room also temporarily houses some glass display cabinets with musical instruments, which will be definitively located in the rooms now being prepared in the new Luigi Cherubini Conservatory Museum.

The works

1. ANDREA DEL SARTO
Christ as the Man of Sorrows
c. 1525
Detached fresco
182x113 cm
Inv. 1890 no. 8675

2. RIDOLFO DEL GHIRLANDAIO
*Removal of the body
of St. Zanobius
St. Zanobius revives a boy*
c. 1516
Oil on wood
203x175 cm (each)
Inv. 1890 nos. 1589, 1584

3. MARIOTTO ALBERTINELLI
Annunciation
1510
Oil on wood
335x230 cm
Inv. 1890 no. 8643

4. FRANCIABIGIO
*Virgin with Child, St. Joseph
and the infant St. John*
c. 1500-1510
Oil on wood
diam. 94 cm
Inv. 1890 no. 888

5. FRANCESCO GRANACCI
Assumption of the Virgin and Saints
c. 1510
Oil on wood
301.5x217.3 cm
Inv. 1890 no. 8650

6. FRA BARTOLOMEO
*The Prophet Isaiah
The Prophet Job*
c. 1514-1516
Oil on wood
168x108 cm (each)
Inv. 1890 nos. 1448, 1449

**7. PIETRO PERUGINO
AND GERINO DA PISTOIA**
*Christ on the Cross between
the Virgin and St. Jerome*
c. 1497-1505
Oil on wood
281x174 cm
Inv. 1890 no. 8733

8. FRANCESCO BOTTICINI
*St. Monica
St. Augustine*
1471
Oil on wood
171x51 cm (each)
Inv. 1890 nos. 8626, 8625

9. FRANCESCO GRANACCI
Virgin of the Girdle
c. 1500-1520
Oil on wood
300x181 cm
Inv. 1890 no. 1596

10. FRANCESCO GRANACCI
Virgin with Child and Saints
c. 1510
Oil on wood
192.5x174 cm
Inv. 1890 no. 3247

11. MARIOTTO ALBERTINELLI
The Holy Trinity
c. 1510
Oil on wood
232x132 cm
Inv. 1890 no. 8660

12. RIDOLFO DEL GHIRLANDAIO
Virgin with Child and Saints
1503
Oil on wood
156x140 cm
Inv. 1890 no. 4652

13. PIETRO PERUGINO
Assumption of the Virgin
1500
Oil on wood
415x246 cm
Inv. 1890 no. 8366

**14. FILIPPINO LIPPI
AND PIETRO PERUGINO**
Deposition
1504 and 1507
Oil on wood
334x225 cm
Inv. 1890 no. 8370

15. GIOVANNI ANTONIO SOGLIANI
*Dispute concerning
the Immaculate Conception*
c. 1530
Oil on wood
347x230 cm
Inv. 1890 no. 3203

In the center of the room:

16. GIAMBOLOGNA
Rape of the Sabine women
1582
Plaster cast
Height 410 cm
Sculptures Inv. no. 1071

1

ANDREA DEL SARTO
Christ as the Man of Sorrows

This fresco was removed in 1810 from the top of the staircase leading to the novitiate in the Santissima Annunziata Monastery in Florence. Despite the poor condition of the work (perhaps also due to the detachment procedure which presented greater risks in that period than today) the figure of the suffering Christ, his pierced hands resting wearily on the stone of the tomb, still expresses the drama of death and pain with great intensity.

2

RIDOLFO DEL GHIRLANDAIO
St. Zanobius revives a boy
Removal of the body of St. Zanobius

These two paintings were commissioned in 1516 by the Compagnia di San Zanobi, headquartered in the presbytery of Santa Maria del Fiore, to complete the decoration of the altar over which Mariotto Albertinelli's *Annunciation* ❸ had already been placed in 1510. Since these two paintings were smaller it is probable that they were hung on the side walls of the area housing the altar and probably inserted in architectural frames. The pathetic expressions of the faces, individual and naturalistic, the clear, limpid forms and the essential lines of the composition are distinctive features of Ridolfo's style, which finds its maximum expression here.

The two paintings were transferred from the storage deposit of the Cenacolo di San Salvi to the Accademia Gallery, where they again hang beside Albertinelli's panel.

6

FRA BARTOLOMEO
The Prophet Isaiah (on the left)
The Prophet Job (on the right)

These two recently restored panels came from the Billi Chapel in the Basilica of Santissima Annunziata in Florence. At their centre was the *Salvator Mundi and the four Evangelists*, today on show in the Palatina Gallery. Cardinal Car-

lo de' Medici purchased the three panels in 1631 and placed them in the Medici house in Piazza San Marco. In 1697 Prince Ferdinand took the central altarpiece to Palazzo Pitti as part of his personal collection, while the two Prophets were passed on to the Uffizi and then to the Accademia. The two Prophets were painted by Fra Bartolomeo immediately after his journey to Rome (c. 1514-1516), and are evidence of his meditations on Michelangelo's Sistine Chapel.

·PETRVS·PERVSINVS·PINXIT·A·D·M·CCCC·

13

PIETRO PERUGINO
Assumption of the Virgin

This altarpiece was located on the high altar of the church in the Benedictine Monastery of Vallombrosa. Perugino painted it with a expert technique using structures and drawings already tested on other, similar great compositions, and dwelling in his usual pleasant way on the decorative details like the Archangel Michael's sophisticated armour on the extreme right.

14

FILIPPINO LIPPI
E PIETRO PERUGINO
Deposition

This painting was part of a grand wooden group commissioned by the friars of Santissima An-nunziata of Florence. Filippino Lippi began work on it in 1504 and finished the upper part except for the body of Christ; he then died, and the work was completed in 1507 by Perugino who also painted the other panels to be inser-ted in the complex structure.

15

GIOVANNI ANTONIO SOGLIANI
Dispute concerning the Immaculate Conception

This panel shows the Doctors of the Church gathered around the body of Adam discussing the question of the Immaculate Conception of the Virgin, a theme also depicted in Carlo Portelli's panel. This work belongs to the specific historical period in which the Catholic Church was particularly intent on consolidating the Marian cult against diffusion of the Lutheran heresy.

16

GIAMBOLOGNA
Rape of the Sabine women

This is the plaster model for the marble sculptured group which can be seen under Loggia dei Lanzi in Piazza della Signoria. Giambologna's virtuosity here ventures to create for the first time a large-sized marble sculpture with a tightly-knit group of three figures, which almost form a single body, in a circular spiral movement seemingly without beginning or end.

When the group was sculpted (1582) it did not have a definite subject but was presented by the artist as a simple exercise in skill; only later was it given the title *Rape of the Sabine women*.

Side wings of the Tribuna

Since the beginning of the 1980s this area has housed a series of works by artists who were contemporaries of Michelangelo, or slightly later. Among these are some of Alessandro Allori's large panels.

The works

1. **FRANCESCO GRANACCI** (below)
Martyrdom of St. Apollonia
c. 1530
Oil on wood
40x59 cm
Inv. 1890 no. 8692

Disputation of St. Catherine of Alexandria
c. 1530
Oil on wood
41x61 cm
Inv. 1890 no. 8691

Martyrdom of St. Catherine
c. 1530
Oil on wood
41x61 cm
Inv. 1890 no. 8690

A Saint before the judge
c. 1530
Oil on wood
39x55 cm
Inv. 1890 no. 8694

The martyrdom of a Saint
c. 1530
Oil on wood
39x55 cm
Inv. 1890 no. 8693

The martyrdom of a Saint
c. 1530
Oil on wood
39x55 cm
Inv. 1890 no. 8695

2. **RIDOLFO DEL GHIRLANDAIO** (above)
Three Angels turning to left
Three Angels turning to right
1508
Oil on wood
111x54 cm (each)
Inv. 1890 nos. 8649, 8648

3. **GIULIANO BUGIARDINI** (above)
Virgin with Child and the infant St. John
1520
Oil on wood
117x88 cm
Inv. 1890 no. 3121

4. **ALESSANDRO ALLORI**
Baptism of Christ
1591
Oil on wood
166x98 cm
Inv. 1890 no. 2175

5. **AGNOLO BRONZINO**
Deposition from the Cross
1561
Oil on wood
355x233.5 cm
Inv. 1890 no. 3491

6. **ALESSANDRO ALLORI**
Annunciation
1603
Oil on canvas
165x103 cm
Dep. Inv. no. 131

7. **MICHELE DI RIDOLFO DEL GHIRLANDAIO**
Portrait of a young woman
c. 1550-1575
Oil on wood
74x54.5 cm
Inv. 1890 no. 6072

8. **JACOPO PONTORMO**
Venus and Cupid
c. 1535
Oil on wood
127x191 cm
Inv. 1890 no. 1570

9. **MICHELE DI RIDOLFO DEL GHIRLANDAIO**
Portrait of a young woman
c. 1550-1575
Oil on wood
74x54.5 cm
Inv. 1890 no. 6070

10. **ALESSANDRO ALLORI**
Virgin and Child with Saints
1575
Oil on wood
411x289 cm
Inv. 1890 no. 3182

11. **STEFANO PIERI**
The sacrifice of Abraham
1585
Oil on canvas
249x160 cm
Inv. 1890 no. 2133

12. **PIER FRANCESCO FOSCHI**
Virgin and Child with the infant St. John
c. 1525-1535
Oil on wood
97x78 cm
Inv. 1890 no. 235

13. **ALESSANDRO ALLORI**
Annunciation
c. 1578-1579
Oil on wood
445x285 cm
Inv. 1890 no. 8662

14. **CECCHINO SALVIATI**
Virgin with Child, infant St. John and Angel
c. 1540-1550
Oil on wood
104x82 cm
Inv. 1890 no. 6065

15. **MASO DA SAN FRIANO**
The Holy Trinity and Saints
c. 1565
Oil on wood
294x170 cm
Inv. 1890 no. 2118

16. **ALESSANDRO ALLORI**
Coronation of the Virgin
1593
Oil on canvas and wood
413x283 cm
Inv. 1890 no. 3171

17. **MICHELE DI RIDOLFO DEL GHIRLANDAIO**
St. Barbara
c. 1550-1577
Oil on canvas
198x156 cm
Inv. 1890 no. 5868

18. **ANONYMOUS FLORENTINE**
Allegory of Strength
c. 1550-1599
Oil on wood
187x142.5 cm
Inv. 1890 no. 8024

19. **COSIMO GAMBERUCCI**
St. Peter healing the lame
1599
Oil on wood
408x260 cm
Inv. 1890 no. 4631

20. **IL POPPI**
Allegorical Figure
c. 1572-1573
Oil on wood
129x103 cm
Inv. 1890 no. 9287

21. **CARLO PORTELLI**
Dispute concerning the Immaculate Conception
1566
Oil on wood
410x248 cm
Inv. 1890 no. 4630

22. **STEFANO PIERI**
Deposition
1587
Oil on wood
171x127 cm
Inv. 1890 no. 1595

23. **SANTI DI TITO**
Jesus entering Jerusalem
c. 1569-1579
Oil on wood
350x230 cm
Inv. 1890 no. 8667

24. **SANTI DI TITO**
Christ's deposition from the Cross with the Virgin, St. John the Baptist, St. Catherine of Alexandria and the donor
c. 1590
Oil on wood
200x168 cm
Inv. 1890 no. 4637

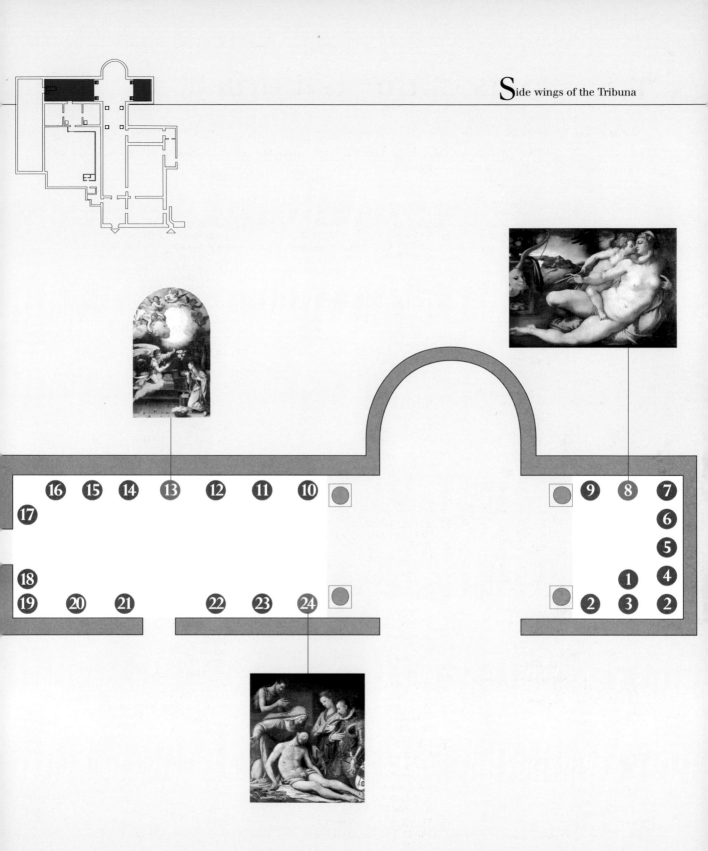

8

JACOPO PONTORMO
Venus and Cupid

This painting was made executed in 1535 by Jacopo Carrucci, known as Pontormo, from a cartoon drawn by Michelangelo, as can be seen from the sculptural forms of Venus and Cupid.

Venus' nudity was covered presumably only a short while after she was painted, because she appears already dressed in the copy by Vasari which can today be seen in Palazzo Colonna in Rome. The painting was restored to its original condition by Ulisse Forni in 1852, revealing Pontormo's nude.

❿❸ ALESSANDRO ALLORI
Annunciation

This panel was commissioned by Sister Laura de' Pazzi in 1578-1579 for the Convent of Montedomini, in whose church it was situated when the holy institution was suppressed and its furnishings confiscated by the State.

The severe and contained composition, suitable for a convent in a time of Counter-reform, is softened by the charming still-life of the basket with clothes and the delicate flowers scattered on the floor.

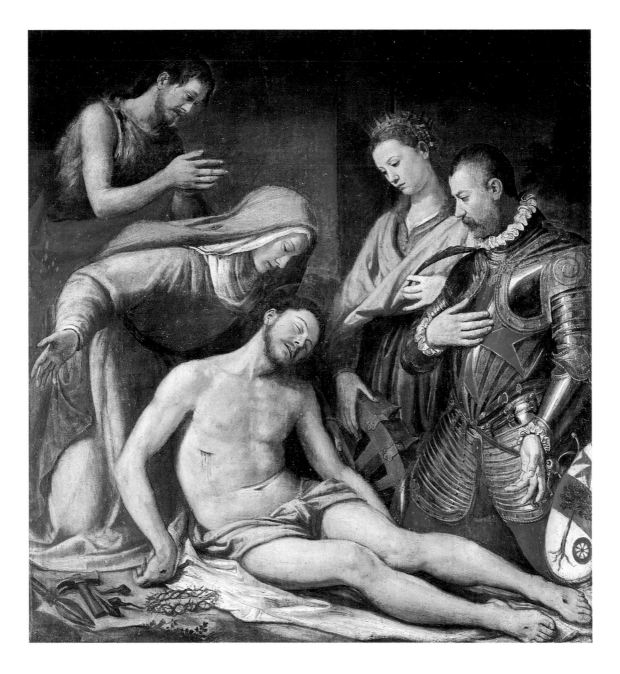

24

SANTI DI TITO
Christ's deposition from the Cross

The painting shows Christ removed from the Cross surrounded by the Virgin, St. John the Baptist, St. Catherine and a messenger wearing armour decorated with the insignia of the knights of St. Stephen.

Despite various attempts by experts, the identity of this last figure has never been established with any certainty.
The chromatic sensitivity of this painting tends to date the work at the beginning of the last decade of the Sixteenth century, the period in which Santi di Tito was most greatly influenced by Cigoli's emphasis on chromatic effects.

Nineteenth Century Room

The large Nineteenth Century Room was conceived and realised in order to provide the collection of plaster casts by Lorenzo Bartolini with a stable and definitive location. However the intention was also to offer the visitor tangible evidence of the Nineteenth century academic origins of this Gallery, today mainly known for Michelangelo's David.

The works
A. The sculptures

1. LORENZO BARTOLINI
Monument to Elisa Baciocchi
1820
Plaster model
Height 211 cm
Sculptures Inv. no. 1181

2. LORENZO BARTOLINI
Titian's Venus
c. 1821
Plaster model
Height 61 cm
Sculptures Inv. no. 1313

3. LORENZO BARTOLINI
Grape harvester
c. 1816-1820
Plaster model
Height 133 cm
Sculptures Inv. no. 1216

4. LORENZO BARTOLINI
Venus
c. 1817
Plaster model
Height 162 cm
Sculptures Inv. no. 1212

5. LORENZO BARTOLINI
Juno
c. 1833
Plaster model
Height 172 cm
Sculptures Inv. no. 1202

6. LORENZO BARTOLINI
*Allegorical figures
for the Demidoff Monument*
1828-1850:
Recognition
Plaster cast
Height 106 cm
Sculptures Inv. no. 1209
Recognition
Plaster model
Height 108 cm
Sculptures Inv. no. 1221
Siberia
Plaster model
Height 220 cm
Sculptures Inv. no. 1174
Charity
Plaster model
Height 190 cm
Sculptures Inv. no. 1175
Nature unveiling herself to Art
Plaster model
Height 220 cm
Sculptures Inv. no. 1176
The Muse of Festivities
Plaster model
Height 190 cm
Sculptures Inv. no. 1177

7. LORENZO BARTOLINI
Emma and Julia Campbell
c. 1819-1820
Plaster model
Height 157 cm
Sculptures Inv. no. 1183

8. LORENZO BARTOLINI
Niccolò Machiavelli
c. 1845
Plaster model
Height 210 cm
Sculptures Inv. no. 1201

9. LORENZO BARTOLINI
Bacchante
1834
Plaster model
Length 154 cm
Sculptures Inv. no. 1204

10. LORENZO BARTOLINI
Nymph of the Scorpion
Before 1837
Plaster model
Height 80 cm
Sculptures Inv. no. 1222

11. LORENZO BARTOLINI
Nymph of the Serpent
Before 1840
Plaster model
Height 121 cm
Sculptures Inv. no. 1203

12. LORENZO BARTOLINI
The table of Cupids
Before 1845
Plaster model
Diameter 125 cm
Sculptures Inv. no. 1220

13. LUIGI PAMPALONI
Innocence
1831
Plaster model
Height 64 cm
Sculptures Inv. no. 1236

14. LUIGI PAMPALONI
Monument to Virginia de Blasis
1839
Plaster model
Height 145 cm
Sculptures Inv. no. 1239

15. LUIGI PAMPALONI
Boy with a dog
1827
Plaster model
Height 58 cm
Sculptures Inv. no. 1237

16. LORENZO BARTOLINI
*Fraternal rivalry
(Lady Bingham's sons)*
Before 1847
Plaster model
Height 66 cm
Sculptures Inv. no. 1257

17. LORENZO BARTOLINI
Monument to Leon Battista Alberti
After 1838
Plaster model
Height 224 cm
Sculptures Inv. no. 1180

18. FRANCESCO POZZI
Bacchante with Faunus and panther
1818
Plaster model
Height 115 cm
Without Inv.

19. LUIGI PAMPALONI
*Monument to Maria
Radzwill Krasinski
with the son Zygmunt*
1839-1841
Plaster model
110x200 cm
Sculptures Inv. nos. 1241,
1242, 1242 bis

20. LUIGI PAMPALONI
Cupid lying in wait
After 1833
Plaster model
Height 108 cm
Sculptures Inv. no. 1234

21. LUIGI PAMPALONI
Cupid with a Swan
After 1834
Plaster model
Height 86 cm
Sculptures Inv. no. 1232

22. LUIGI PAMPALONI
Chloe
1834
Plaster model
Height 74 cm
Sculptures Inv. no. 1233

23. BARTOLINIAN SCHOOL
Nymph
c. 1840-1850
Plaster model
Height 128 cm
Sculptures Inv. no. 1215

24. LORENZO BARTOLINI
Monument to Sofia Zamoiska
1838-1844
Plaster cast
Length 187 cm
Sculptures Inv. no. 1314

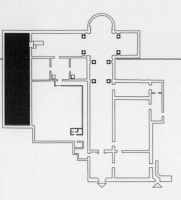

25. LORENZO BARTOLINI
Cupid
After 1841
Plaster model
Height 118 cm
Sculptures Inv. no. 1253

26. LORENZO BARTOLINI
Narcissus
c. 1830-1850
Plaster model
Height 172 cm
Sculptures Inv. no. 1218

27. LORENZO BARTOLINI
*Monument to Vittorio
Fossombroni*
1846
Plaster model
Height 93 cm
Sculptures Inv. nos. 1227,
1228, 1192

28. ULISSE CAMBI
Daphnes and Chloe
1834
Plaster model
Height 145 cm
Dep. Inv. no. 72

29. ULISSE CAMBI
Aconzio
1835
Plaster model
Height 148 cm
Dep. Inv. no. 74

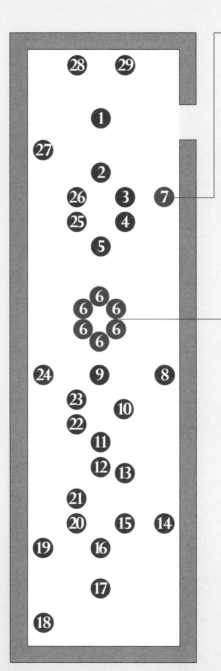

B. The paintings

30. IRENE DUCLOS PARENTI
*Copy of Andrea del Sarto's
"Virgin of the Sack"*
1775
Oil on canvas
181x385 cm
Without Inv.

31. LUIGI MUSSINI
Sacred Music
1841
Oil on canvas
150x104 cm
Acc. Inv. no. 292/C.G.1

32. FRANCESCO SABATELLI
Copy of Titian's "Assunta"
1827
Oil on canvas
250x145 cm
Without Inv.

33. FRANCESCO NENCI
*Oedipus freed from his bindings
by a shepherd*
1817
Oil on canvas
218x152 cm
Gen. Cat. no. 5

34. CESARE MUSSINI
The death of Atala
1830
Oil on canvas
225x273 cm
Gen. Cat. no. 16

35. ANTONIO PUCCINELLI (below)
The Hebrews in Babylonia
1851
Oil on canvas
67.5x133 cm
Without Inv.

36. ANTONIO PUCCINELLI (above)
*An episode from the slaughter
of the Innocents*
1852
Oil on canvas
200x145 cm
Gen. Cat. no. 21

37. GIUSEPPE FATTORI
The Baptist admonishing Herod
c. 1856
Oil on canvas
282x357 cm
Acc. Inv. no. 461

38. RAFFAELLO SORBI (below)
Death of Corso Donati
1861
Oil on canvas
136x176 cm
Without Inv.

39. EUGENIO PRATI (above)
*Michelangelo to whom
Zuccari presents Barocci*
1868
Oil on canvas
174x136 cm
Without Inv.

40. BENEDETTO SERVOLINI
Death of Filippo Strozzi
1833
Oil on canvas
300x410 cm
Gen. Cat. no. 614

41. DEMOSTENE MACCIÒ
*Fra Benedetto da Fojano
in prison*
c. 1867
Oil on canvas
147x203 cm
Acc. Inv. no. 431

42. BENEDETTO SERVOLINI
Orlando captures a horse
1834
Oil on canvas
300x545 cm
Gen. Cat. no. 613

43. BALDASSARE CALAMAI (below)
*Dante visiting the Inferno
accompanied by Virgil
recognizes Farinata*
1825
Oil on canvas
191x153 cm
Without Inv.

44. GIUSEPPE COLIGNON
(above)
The beheading of the Baptist
c. 1860
Oil on canvas
103x123 cm
Acc. Inv. no. 338

45. SILVESTRO LEGA
(below)
*David calms Saul's
fury with the harp*
1852
Oil on canvas
133x174 cm
Without Inv.

46. LUIGI MUSSINI (above)
*The giving of alms according
to evangelical Charity
and according to worldly
Ostentation*
1844
Oil on canvas
116x147 cm
Acc. Inv. no. 383

47. CESARE MUSSINI (below)
*Francis I at the bedside
of the dying Leonardo*
1828
Oil on canvas
145x172 cm
G.A.M. Dep. no. 53

48. LEOPOLDO NEOFRESCHI (above)
*Alessandro Magno about to drink
from a poisoned cup*
1794
Oil on canvas
Measurements are not available
Without Inv.

JACOPO PONTORMO
*Ward in the San Matteo
Hospital*
c. 1513-1514
Detached fresco
91x150 cm
Inv. 1890 no. 9385

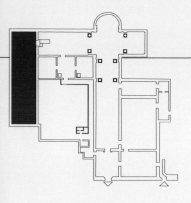

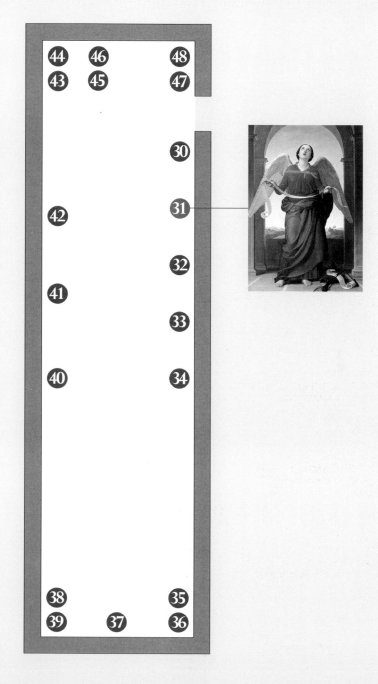

6

LORENZO BARTOLINI
Demidoff Monument

The commemorative monument to count Nikolaj Demidoff was commissioned by his sons Paul and Anatolij in 1828, on the death of their father.
Several times interrupted and restarted when the difficulties were overcome, it was only placed where it stands today (in Piazza Demidoff, opposite Lungarno Serristori, in Florence) in 1871.
The work was finished by Romanelli, a pupil of Bartolini who took over his workshop.
It was a grand and complex project, consisting of many statues, some larger than life, with complicated allegorical meaning.
The plaster model of the central group, depicting the count Nikolaj with his son Anatolij, has been lost.

7

LORENZO BARTOLINI
Emma and Julia Campbell

A visit to Bartolini's studio by Lady Barry, an English author who admired his work, procured the artist several commissions from the British aristocracy. Among these was the portrait of the Campbell sisters portrayed in the act of dancing commissioned by their mother Lady Charlotte Campbell, whom the artist met in Florence between September of 1819 and August of 1820. The marble original is thought to be in the dining room of the Inveraray Castle, the property of the Duke of Argyll in Scotland. Although this work is still dominated by neo-classical taste, it reveals Bartolini's early purist orientation during these years. The two girls are portrayed "in antique style", wearing sandals and classical tunics bound under the breast by narrow ribbons. On this group traces of the so-called "dots" procedure, used to mark the angles and the various depths of the points to be reproduced on the block of marble, can be detected.

31

LUIGI MUSSINI
Sacred Music

This is one of the pictures which testify to the original bond between the Accademia Gallery and the School of Accademia delle Belle Arti. Luigi Mussini painted it in Rome in 1841 as an trial for his academic pension.

In that same year it was exhibited in the Prize-winners Gallery of the Florence Accademia, where it remained for years.

The picture represents a youth with wings gazing upward toward heaven, her lips parted in

a liturgical chant. *Sacred Music* is a clear and illustrious example of Purism in Tuscany, and of how Mussini shared in the experience of the Nazarenes who drew inspiration from great examples of Fifteenth and Sixteenth centuries painting.

Luigi Mussini had also the chance to learn stylistic rigor in drawing directly from Ingres, who stayed in Florence for some time in the 1820s.

Thirteenth and Early Fourteenth C. Room

The Florentine Gothic painting route (in three rooms) starts in this room, which house many gold-leaf background panels in an absolutely unique collection of its kind. Displayed in the central room are works by artists predating Giotto or his contemporaries, like the Master of San Gaggio and Pacino di Buonaguida; in the right-hand room are Giotto's direct followers, Taddeo Gaddi, Bernardo Daddi, Jacopo del Casentino; in the left-hand room are the Orcagnas and their close collaborators.

The works

1. FLORENTINE PAINTER
Painted Cross
1280-1299
Tempera on wood
296x197 cm
Inv. 1890 no. 1345

2. PACINO DI BUONAGUIDA
Crucifixion and Saints
c. 1319-1320
Tempera on wood
126x243 cm
Inv. 1890 n. 8568

3. PACINO DI BUONAGUIDA
The Tree of Life
c. 1305-1310
Tempera on wood
248x151 cm
Inv. 1890 no. 8459

4. PACINO DI BUONAGUIDA
Virgin and Child
c. 1320-1339
Tempera on wood
75x46 cm
Inv. 1890 no. 6146

5. PACINO DI BUONAGUIDA
St. Nicolas
St. John the Evangelist
St. Proculous
c. 1310-1320
Tempera on wood
75x52 cm (each)
Inv. 1890 nos. 8698, 8699, 8700

6. MASTER OF THE MAGDALENE
*The repentant Magdalene
and eight scenes from her life*
c. 1280-1285
Tempera on wood
164x76 cm
Inv. 1890 no. 8466

7. MASTER OF THE MAGDALENE
*St. John the Evangelist
and scenes from his life;
St. James and scenes
from his life*
c. 1250-1290
Tempera on wood
67x60 cm (each)
Dep. Inv. nos. 121, 122

8. MASTER OF ST. CECILIA
Enthroned Virgin and Child
c. 1310-1320
Tempera on wood
185x97 cm
Inv. 1890 no. 5917

**9. MASTER OF THE
CORSI CRUCIFIX**
*Christ Crucified among mourners
and the genuflecting donor*
In the moulding:
The Mystic Pelican
c. 1315
Tempera on wood
259x235 cm
Inv. 1890 no. 436

10. MASTER OF SAN GAGGIO
*The Virgin and Child
with Saints*
c. 1300-1310
Tempera on wood
259x235 cm
Inv. 1890 no. 6115

11. ANONYMOUS TUSCAN
*The Virgin and Child
with two Angels*
c. 1250-1260
Tempera on wood
130x73 cm
Inv. 1890 no. 433

12. ANONYMOUS TUSCAN
Enthroned Virgin and Child
c. 1270-1275
Tempera on wood
125x73 cm
Inv. 1890 no. 435

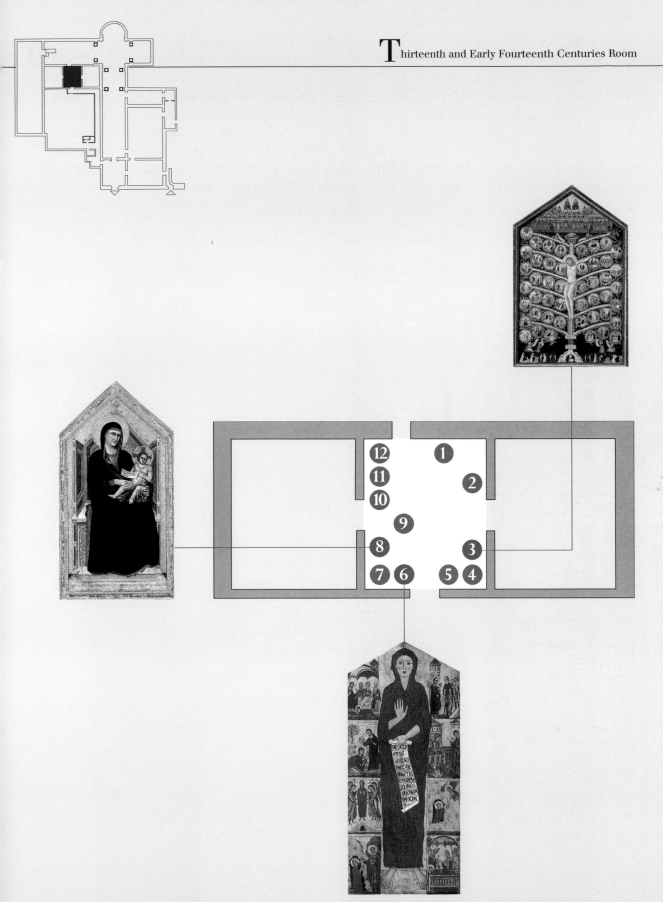

3

PACINO DI BUONAGUIDA
The Tree of Life

With its vivid colours and sophisticated drawing (Pacino was also a famous illuminator),
this painting mainly illustrates the content of
St. Bonaventure's *Lignum Vitae*, although there are also many scenes and scrolls alluding to
biblical texts. In its entirety it appears as a large
doctrinal page for meditation as well as an image to be admired.
The subject of the illustration is the genealo-
gy of Christ, who is shown nailed to the tree-
shaped cross with its roots on a rocky moun-
tain, symbolising Mount Calvary.

6

MASTER OF THE MAGDALENE
*The repentant Magdalene
and eight scenes from her life*

This panel, coming from the Convento della Santissima Annunziata, clearly exemplifies Florentine painting before Giotto, within whose circle this anonymous painter can be placed. The Master of the Magdalene set up one of the most pro-

ductive studio in Florence (1265-1290), and shows evidence of attention to the innovations introduced by Cimabue. In this sense, the small side scenes, which offer a direct and lively narrative of moments from the Saint's life, are more attractive than the solemn central figure. A conspicuous example are the naturalistic landscape elements in the background of the *Noli me tangere* (depicted in the second scene on the left).

8

MASTER OF THE ST. CECILIA
Enthroned Virgin and Child

Exhibited from 1902 to 1998 in the Museo Civico of Pescia, this painting is a work fundamental for the history of Fourteenth century Florentine painting. It is attributed to an anonymous contemporary and collaborator of Giotto, whose hand is recognisable also in some parts of the frescoes with *Scenes from the life of St. Francis* in the upper Basilica of Assisi.

Giottesque Room

The works

1. JACOPO DEL CASENTINO
St. Bartholomew and Angels
1330-1340
Tempera on wood
266x122 cm
Inv. 1890 no. 440

2. JACOPO DEL CASENTINO
St. Egidius
St. John the Baptist
St. John the Evangelist
In the cuspids:
Prophets
1325-1335
Tempera on wood
118x43 cm
Inv. 1890 nos. 8571, 8572, 8573

3. MASTER OF THE DOMINICAN EFFIGIES
Virgin with Child
and Saints
Coronation of the Virgin
and Saints
c. 1325-1350
Tempera on wood
54x196 cm (each)
Inv. 1890 nos. 4633, 4634

4. PUCCIO DI SIMONE
Virgin of Humility and Saints
c. 1346-1358
Tempera on wood
132x191 cm
Inv. 1890 no. 8569

5. BERNARDO DADDI
Crucifixion
St. Christopher
In the back:
c. 1340-1348
Tempera on wood
40x17 cm
Inv. 1890 no. 8563

6. BERNARDO DADDI
St. Bartholomew
St. Lawrence
c. 1340
Tempera on wood
109x40 cm (each)
Inv. 1890 nos. 8706, 8707

7. BERNARDO DADDI
Crucifixion
1343
Tempera on wood
124x157 cm
Inv. 1890 no. 8570

8. BERNARDO DADDI
Coronation of the Virgin
with Angels and 42 Saints
1340-1348
Tempera on wood
186x270 cm
Inv. 1890 no. 3449

9. BERNARDO DADDI
The Crucifix with the Virgin
and St. John
c. 1348
Tempera on wood
350x275 cm
Inv. 1890 no. 442

10. BERNARDO DADDI
Crucifixion with four Angels,
the Virgin, the Magdalene
and St. John the Evangelist
In the wings side:
PUCCIO DI SIMONE
St. Mary Magdalene,
St. Michael Archangel,
St. Julian, St. Martha
c. 1346-1348
Tempera on wood
102x46 cm (total)
Inv. 1890 nos. 443, 6140

11. BERNARDO DADDI
Virgin with Child and Saints,
Crucifixion; The Knights of Death,
Legend of the three Live Men and
three Dead Men
c. 1330-1348
Tempera on wood
35x24 cm; 19x24 cm
Inv. 1890 nos. 8566, 8567, 6152, 6153

12. TADDEO GADDI
(Reliquaries Cabinet)
Scenes from the Life of Christ
and of St. Francis
c. 1330-1335
Tempera on wood
41x29.5 cm; 41x36.5 cm (panels)
72x158 cm (lunette)
Inv. 1890 from no. 8581 to no. 8603

13. TADDEO GADDI
Virgin with Child
St. John the Baptist and St. Peter
In the cuspids:
Announcing Angel
Our Lady of the Annunciation
c. 1330-1345
Tempera on wood
48x30 cm (entire)
Inv. 1890 no. 3144

14. TADDEO GADDI
Virgin with Child,
Saints and Prophets
c. 1330-1350
In the lunette:
NICCOLÒ DI PIETRO GERINI (?)
Benediction of Christ and two
Prophets
In the predella:
NICCOLÒ DI PIETRO GERINI (?)
Christ as the Man of Sorrows
with the Virgin and Saints
c. 1390-1410
Tempera on wood
183x127 cm (total)
Inv. 1890 no. 448

15. TADDEO GADDI
Enthroned Virgin and Child
c. 1330-1335
Tempera on wood
52x26 cm
Dep. Inv. no. 164

16. BERNARDO DADDI (above)
Enthroned Virgin with Child
between two Angels, St. John
the Baptist and St. Luke
1333
Tempera on wood
219x132 cm
Inv. 1890 no. 6170

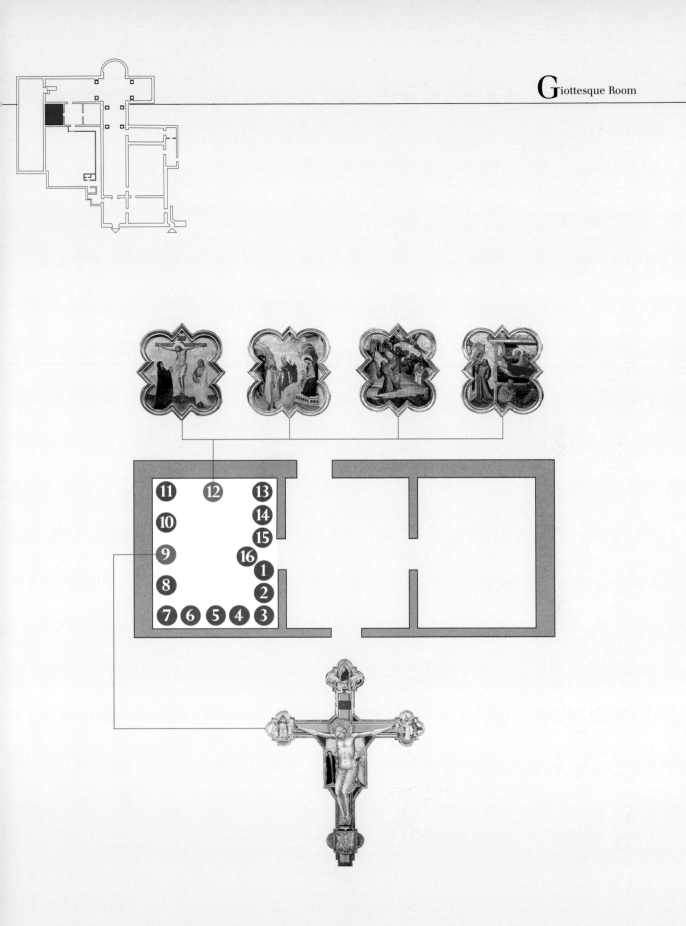

9

BERNARDO DADDI
Crucifix with the Virgin and St. John

This large, shaped *Crucifix* (c. 1348) possibly comes from the Florentine Church of San Donato in Polverosa and was presumably placed above the high altar, hanging from the ceiling. In medieval churches this type of image was often placed on top of the iconostasis, i.e. the dividing wall between the presbytery and the choir, as is clearly shown in the Greccio nativity scene painted by Giotto in the Basilica of St. Francis in Assisi.

12

TADDEO GADDI
*Scenes from the Life of Christ
and of St. Francis*

These panels (c. 1333) came from the sacristy of the Basilica of Santa Croce where they decorated wooden furniture, perhaps a reliquary cupboard. The single episodes from the life of St. Francis are illustrated in a parallel with the Life of Christ: for example, the episode with the *Imposition of the stigmata to St. Francis* corresponds to the *Crucifixion*. Giotto's most direct pupil, Taddeo was the first to include his master's innovations: note the solid volumetric disposition of the figures and the well-constructed architectural perspective, which indicate a *modus operandi* very far removed from the transcendent and ethereal world of Byzantine painting.

Room of the Orcagnas and their followers

The works

1. ANDREA ORCAGNA
*Enthroned Virgin
with Child and Saints*
c. 1355
Tempera on wood
126x204 cm
Inv. 1890 no. 3469

2. ANDREA ORCAGNA
Pentecost
c. 1365
Tempera on wood
194x274 cm
Dep. Inv. no. 165

3. NARDO DI CIONE
*The Trinity; St. Romualdus;
St. John Evangelist*
In the cuspids:
*Angel of the Apocalypse
and two worshipping Angels*
In the predella:
*Scenes from the life
of St. Romualdus*
1365
Tempera on wood
300x210 cm
Inv. 1890 no. 8464

**4. MASTER OF THE ASHMOLEAN
MUSEUM PREDELLA**
*St. Vescovus
St. Lawrence*
c. 1360-1365
Tempera on wood
88x32 cm (each)
Inv. 1890 nos. 8701, 8702

**5. MASTER OF THE
ST. NICCOLÒ ALTAR**
Virgin of Humility and four Angels
c. 1350-1380
Tempera on wood
107x62 cm
Inv. 1890 no. 4698

6. NICCOLÒ DI TOMMASO
*Coronation of the Virgin
with Angels and Saints*
c. 1370-1375
Tempera on wood
85x36 cm
Inv. 1890 no. 8580

7. JACOPO DI CIONE
*Christ Crucified between the Virgin
and St. John with four Angels*
c. 1380-1398
Tempera on wood
244x135 cm
Inv. 1890 no. 4670

8. JACOPO DI CIONE
*Virgin with Child
Crucifixion
Four saints*
In the cuspids: *Annunciation*
c. 1380-1399
Tempera on wood
60x34 cm
Inv. 1890 no. 8465

9. JACOPO DI CIONE
Virgin of Humility
c. 1380
Tempera on wood
105x66 cm
Dep. Inv. no. 132

10. JACOPO DI CIONE
Scenes from Christ's Childhood
c. 1370
Tempera on wood
151x101 cm
Inv. 1890 no. 5887

**11. MASTER
OF THE RINUCCINI CHAPEL**
Vision of St. Bernard and Saints
In the cuspids:
*Benediction of the Redeemer
Annunciation*
In the predella:
Scenes from the life of St. Bernard
c. 1365-1370
Tempera on wood
175x200 cm
Inv. 1890 no. 8463

**12. MASTER
OF THE RINUCCINI CHAPEL**
Charity of St. Anthony abbot
c. 1370-1380
Tempera on wood
39x34 cm
Inv. 1890 no. 460

**13. MASTER
OF THE RINUCCINI CHAPEL**
*St. Michael Archangel,
St. Bartholomew,
St. Julian and the donor*
After 1348
Tempera on wood
158x86 cm
Inv. 1890 no. 6134

14. JACOPO DI CIONE
Coronation of the Virgin
1372
Tempera on wood
350x190 cm
Inv. 1890 no. 456

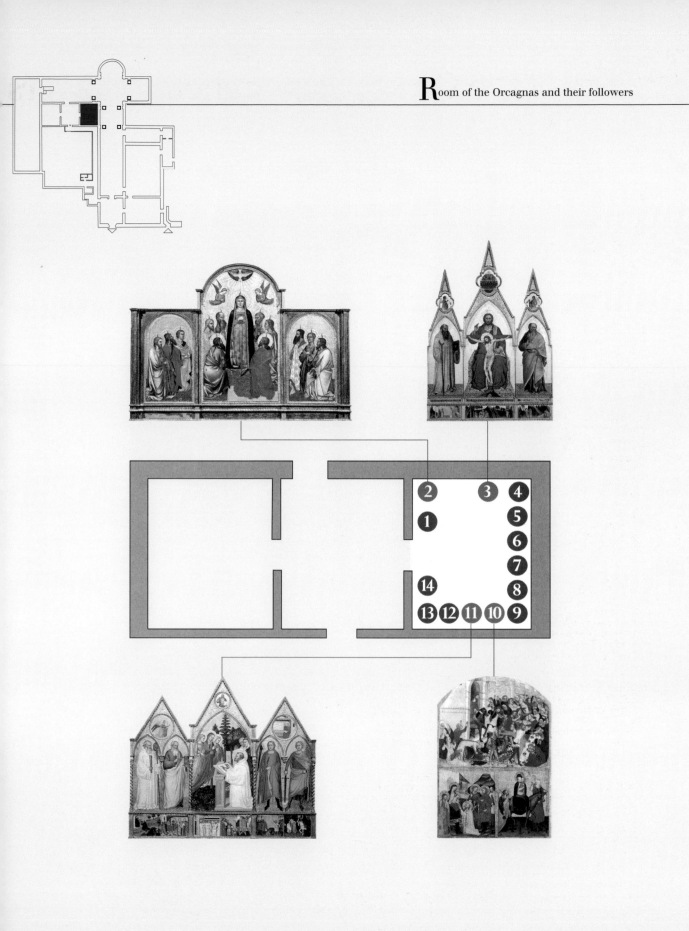

2

ANDREA ORCAGNA
Pentecost

This triptych (c. 1365) reveals the characteristics of Andrea Orcagna's painting style in the last phase of his life; with its square spaces, the rigid frontal arrangement of the figures and the limited chromatic range, it must have fitted harmoniously in the Romanesque Church of the Santi Apostoli in Florence, where it came from. In the second half of the Eighteenth century it was transferred to the Church of Badia, from where it was passed to the Accademia Gallery in 1939. It is likely that Andrea's younger brother Jacopo assisted in the painting work, and his hand can be seen in areas of softer, more blended application of colour in some of the Apostles, and hints of softness in the volumetric construction.

3

NARDO DI CIONE
The Trinity; *St. Romualdus*;
St. John Evangelist

This polyptych was commissioned by Giovanni
Ghiberti for his chapel in the Chapter of Santa
Maria degli Angioli. It was removed and taken
(c. 1750) to the Della Stufa Chapel, dedicated to
St. Andrew, and on this occasion St. John was repainted to resemble St. Andrew. Today the triptych has resumed its original appearance.

10

JACOPO DI CIONE
*Scenes from
Christ's Childhood*

This panel was in the past attributed to an anonymous master known as the Master of Christ's Childhood because of the scenes depicted here, but has
now been included in the early works of Jacopo di
Cione, brother of Andrea Orcagna and quite close
in his lively narrative style to Niccolò di Tommaso.

11

MASTER OF THE RINUCCINI CHAPEL
Vision of St. Bernard and Saints

The panel is the work of a painter who has remained anonymous, and who worked with Giovanni da Milano on the fresco decorations of the Rinuccini Chapel in Santa Croce, completing them when da Milano left Florence. Stylistically it is clearly the work of a painter trained in the Orcagna studio, with its strong sense of volumetric disposition and monumentality. However, contact with the great Lombardian master has influenced his chromatic range making it warmer and brighter compared to the more adherent followers of Orcagna.

Giovanni da Milano Room

These recently restored and rearranged rooms bring together the varied and exhaustive range of late Gothic Florentine painting.
These include portable altarpieces and grand polyptychs, as well as a collection of nine works by Lorenzo Monaco an incomparably beautiful group of exceptional rarity, through which we can become familiar with the work of this great Gothic painter in all the phases of his artistic career.

The works

1. **DON SILVESTRO DE' GHERARDUCCI**
Virgin of Humility and Angels
c. 1370-1375
Tempera on wood
164x89 cm
Inv. 1890 no. 3161

2. **MASTER OF THE ASHMOLEAN MUSEUM PREDELLA**
Virgin and Child
c. 1370-1390
Tempera on wood
diam. 92 cm
Dep. Inv. no. 178

3. **ANDREA DI BONAIUTO**
St. Agnes and St. Domitilla
c. 1365
Tempera on wood
65x56 cm
Inv. 1890 no. 3145

4. **GIOVANNI DA MILANO**
Christ as the Man of Sorrows
1365
Tempera on wood
122x58 cm
Inv. 1890 no. 8467

5. **MASTER OF THE ACCADEMIA MISERICORDIA (GIOVANNI GADDI?)**
Stigmata of St. Francis, Nativity, Conversion of St. Paul
c. 1375
Tempera on wood
50x90 cm
Inv. 1890 no. 8565

6. **MASTER OF THE ACCADEMIA MISERICORDIA (GIOVANNI GADDI?)**
Virgin and Child between St. Peter and St. Paul
c. 1355-1360
Tempera on wood
116x62 cm
Inv. 1890 no. 437

7. **MASTER OF THE ACCADEMIA MISERICORDIA (GIOVANNI GADDI?)**
Virgin of Charity
c. 1380
Tempera on wood
64x35 cm
Inv. 1890 no. 8562

8. **ANONYMOUS FLORENTINE**
Annunciation
In the cuspid:
Two Prophets
In the predella:
Adoration of the shepherds,
Adoration of the Magi,
Presentation at the Temple
Second half XIV century
Tempera on wood
215x116 cm
Inv. 1890 no. 6098

9. **MASTER OF THE ACCADEMIA MISERICORDIA (GIOVANNI GADDI?)**
Enthroned Virgin and Child between two Angels and Saints
c. 1375
Tempera on wood
90x48 cm
Dep. Inv. no. 176

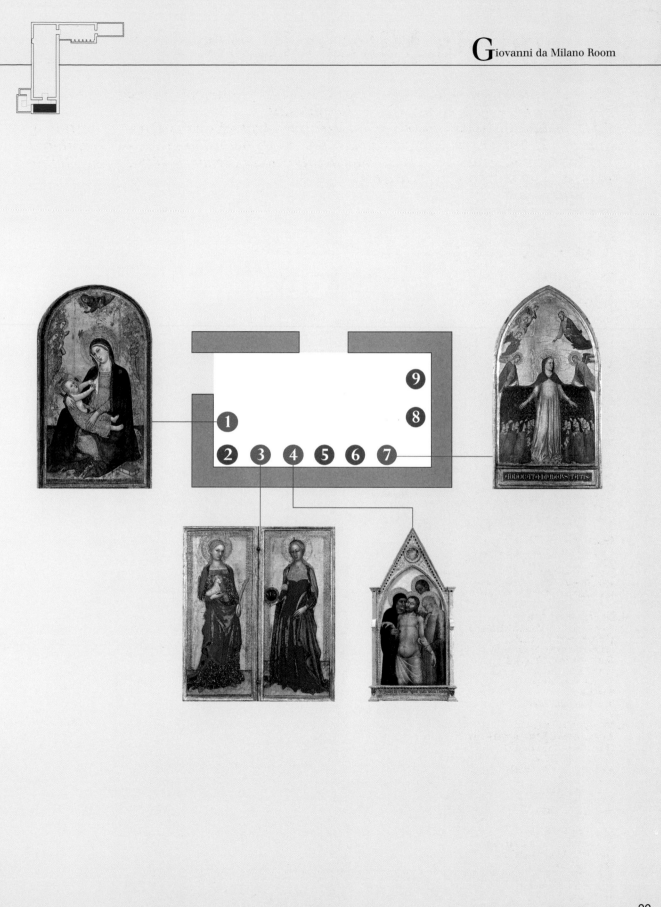

1

DON SILVESTRO DE' GHERARDUCCI
Virgin of Humility and Angels

Silvestro de' Gherarducci entered the Monastery of Santa Maria degli Angioli in 1348 aged nine. He worked with Lorenzo Monaco as a painter and illuminator, never losing the characteristic rich and colourful decorative elements which denote his Sienese origins. The *Virgin of Humility* (c. 1370-1375), which depicts the Virgin sitting on the ground on a cushion, is a subject particularly dear to late Gothic tastes.

3

ANDREA DI BONAIUTO
St. Agnes and St. Domitilla

Andrea di Bonaiuto (also known as Andrea da Firenze), a Florentine painter who trained in the studio of Nardo di Cione, brother of Andrea Orcagna, is famous above all for having frescoed the Spagnuoli Chapel in the Santa Maria Novella Monastery. This small diptych (c. 1365) is stylistically and therefore chronologically close to that work and demonstrates the painter's knowledge and assimilation of the work of Giovanni da Milano, who was present and working in Florence in those very years.

The two female figures shown here particularly stand out for the courtly sophistication of their costly clothes and the intense use of "chiaroscuro".

·Io gouani da myclano depinff questa tauola i mǝ̃ctlbv·

4

GIOVANNI DA MILANO
Christ as the Man of Sorrows

This small devotional panel represents one of the greatest achievements of Fourteenth century painting in Florence after the death of Giotto. It was painted for the Florentine Church of San Girolamo alla Costa, dated 1365 and signed, and at the bottom bears the coats of arms of the Strozzi and Rinieri families who obviously commissioned it. Giovanni da Milano's painting, with its intense sensitivity to colour and moving sentimentality offers an alternative to the severe style of Orcagna, which had dominated the gloomy period following the Great Plague of 1348. With Giovanni's work, Florence opened up to the new insistence of the International Gothic trend.

7

MASTER OF THE ACCADEMIA MISERICORDIA (GIOVANNI GADDI?)
Virgin of Charity

This panel comes from the Augustinian Monastery of Santa Maria in Candeli. It portrays the *Virgin as Mater Misericordiae*, sheltering under her mantle, held up by two angels, twenty-three Augustinian nuns and four women, probably the donors of the tabernacle.

Once considered the work of an anonymous Fifteenth century painter, it is now attributed to a master who takes his name from this painting, to whom several other works in the same room have also been attributed.

The calligraphic elegance and delicate treatment of color seem to indicate that the painter may have worked in illumination as well. It has recently been hypothesized that the Master of the Accademia Misericordia may be Giovanni Gaddi, the elder brother of the more famous Agnolo Gaddi, documented as a painter from 1369-1386.

Late Fourteenth Century Room

The works

1. **LORENZO DI BICCI**
Enthroned St. Martin
In the predella:
Charity of St. Martin
c. 1380-1385
Tempera on wood; 263x99 cm
Dep. Inv. no. 174
Inv. 1890 no. 462 (predella)

2. **NICCOLÒ DI PIETRO GERINI**
*The Holy Trinity with St. Francis
and St. Mary Magdalene*
c. 1380-1385
Tempera on wood; 86x61 cm
Inv. 1890 no. 3944

3. **LORENZO DI BICCI**
St. Julian and St. Zanobius
c. 1380-1400
Tempera on wood
114x70 cm
Inv. 1890 no. 5410

4. **MARIOTTO DI NARDO**
Virgin with Child and Saints
c. 1380-1400
Tempera on wood; 161x118 cm
Inv. 1890 no. 3460

5. **NICCOLÒ DI PIETRO GERINI**
*Crucifixion with St. Francis
in adoration and Saints*
In the cuspids:
Benediction of Christ
and *Annunciation*
c. 1400
Tempera on wood; 208x180 cm
Inv. 1890 no. 3152
In the cuspids:
**AGNOLO DI DOMENICO
DEL MAZZIERE**
The four Evangelists
Early XVI century
Tempera on wood; 105x175 cm
Inv. 1890 no. 5061

6. **SPINELLO ARETINO,
NICCOLÒ DI PIETRO GERINI,
LORENZO DI NICCOLÒ**
*Coronation of the Virgin,
Angels and Saints*
1401
Tempera on wood; 275x278 cm
Inv. 1890 no. 8468

7. **MARIOTTO DI NARDO**
Virgin with Child and Saints
In the cuspid:
Two Angels
c. 1418
Tempera on wood; 225x120 cm
Inv. 1890 no. 473

8. **MARIOTTO DI NARDO**
Annunciation
c. 1400-1410
Tempera on wood; 137x136 cm
Inv. 1890 no. 463

9. **NICCOLÒ DI PIETRO GERINI**
*Enthroned Virgin and Child
among St. Anthony abbot, St. John,
St. Lawrence and St. Julian*
1404
Tempera on wood; 178x264 cm
Inv. 1890 no. 8610

10. **LIPPO D'ANDREA**
*Enthroned Virgin and Child
with Saints*
In the predella:
Scenes from the lives of Saints
and *Nativity*
First half of XV century
Tempera on wood; 190x273 cm
Dep. Inv. no. 18

11. **BICCI DI LORENZO**
*St. Paul; St. Benedict;
St. Giovanni Gualberto; St. Peter*
1430-1435
Tempera on wood; 54x19 cm
Inv. 1890 nos. 5985-5988

12. **NICCOLÒ DI PIETRO GERINI**
*Enthroned Virgin and Child
with Saints*
c. 1400-1410
Tempera on wood; 279x122 cm
Inv. 1890 no. 439

13. **JACOPO CAMBI**
*Coronation of the Virgin between
eight Angels and fourteen Saints*
In the upper border:
*Eleven scenes from the life of the
Virgin delimited by two Prophets
and ten Saints*
1336
Embroidered altar-facing
106x440 cm
18 cm upper border
Ancient fabrics Inv. 1913 no. 881

14. **FLORENTINE PAINTER**
*Virgin of Humility between
two Angels*
c. 1390-1399
Tempera on wood; 80x48 cm
Inv. 1890 no. 465

15. **BICCI DI LORENZO**
*St. Bartholomew; St. Paul;
St. Judas Taddeo (?); St. James;
St. Philip (?); St. Apostle*
c. 1420
Tempera on wood; 49.5x13.5 cm (each)
Inv. 1890 nos. 6141-6143

16. **BICCI DI LORENZO**
*St. Jerome and St. Lawrence
St. Andrew and St. Michael*
c. 1435
Tempera on wood; 145x58 cm (each)
Dep. Inv. no. 12

17. **ROSSELLO DI JACOPO FRANCHI**
*Coronation of the Virgin with Angels
and Saints*
In the cuspid:
*Benediction of the Eternal,
Two Prophets* and *Annunciation*
In the predella:
*Christ as the Man of Sorrows
and Saints*
1420
Tempera on wood; 344x390 cm
Inv. 1890 no. 8460

18. **ROSSELLO DI JACOPO FRANCHI**
*St. Francis
St. John the Baptist*
c. 1400-1410
Tempera on wood
138x67 cm (each)
Inv. 1890 nos. 6103, 6094

19. **GIOVANNI DAL PONTE**
*St. Julian
St. John the Baptist*
c. 1430
Tempera on wood; 138x67 cm (each)
Inv. 1890 nos. 6232, 6105

20. **GIOVANNI DAL PONTE**
*Coronation of the Virgin with four
musical Angels and St. Francis,
St. John the Baptist, St. Ivo
and St. Dominic*
In the cuspid:
*Descent into Limbo
Annunciation*
c. 1420-1430
Tempera on wood; 194x208 cm
Inv. 1890 no. 458

21. **GIOVANNI DAL PONTE**
*St. Helen
St. James the Elder*
1420-1430
Tempera on wood; 94x35 cm (each)
Inv. 1890 nos. 8744, 8746

22. **MASTER
OF BORGO ALLA COLLINA**
*Crucifixion among the Virgin,
St. Francis and kneeling donor*
First half of XV century
Tempera on wood; 60x41 cm
Inv. 1890 no. 3149

23. **SPINELLO ARETINO**
St. Stephen
In the cuspid:
Crucifixion with mourners
c. 1400-1405
Tempera on wood; 93x33 cm
Inv. 1890 no. 6287

24. **NICCOLÒ DI PIETRO GERINI**
*Christ as the Man of Sorrows
with the symbols of Passion*
In the cuspid:
The Redeemer and four Saints
In the predella:
*The funeral of a brother in the
Compagnia del Pellegrino*
1404-1408
Tempera on wood; 358x158 cm
Inv. 1890 nos. 5048, 5067, 5066

25. **NICCOLÒ DI PIETRO GERINI**
Virgin with Child and Saints
Beginning XV century
Tempera on wood; 85.5x50 cm
Inv. 1890 no. 8578

26. **CENNI DI FRANCESCO** (above)
Nativity
c. 1395-1400
Tempera on wood; 144x80 cm
Inv. 1890 no. 6139

27. **MARIOTTO DI NARDO** (below)
*Crucifixion and four Stories
of St. Nicolas*
1410-1415
Tempera on wood; 40x242 cm
Inv. 1890 no. 9206

28. MARIOTTO DI NARDO
Enthroned Virgin with Saints
In the cuspids:
Annunciation and *Crucifixion*
In the predella:
Stories of the Virgin
c. 1390-1395
Tempera on wood
165x242 cm (central part)
42x267 cm (predella)
Inv. 1890 nos. 8612, 8613,
3260, 3258, 3259

29. LORENZO DI NICCOLÒ
*Coronation of the Virgin with
four musical Angels*;
St. Bartholomew and *St. Zanobius*
c. 1400-1410
Tempera on wood
151.4x159 cm
Inv. 1890 nos. 4656, 6087, 6088

30. SPINELLO ARETINO
*Enthroned Virgin and Child and
four Angels with St. Paolino,
St. John the Baptist, St. Andrew
and St. Matthew Evangelist*
1391
Tempera on wood; 174x210 cm
Inv. 1890 no. 8461

31. "FRANCESCO"
*Virgin and Child between two
Angels and two Saints*
In the cuspid: *Benediction of Christ*
In the predella: *Christ teaching*
1391
Tempera on wood; 210x100 cm
Inv. 1890 no. 6154

32. GIOVANNI DEL BIONDO
Annunciation
In the cuspids:
*Christ at the Column,
Crucifixion* and *Resurrection*
In the predella:
*Christ as the Man of Sorrows
between mourners and Saints*
c. 1380
Tempera on wood; 406x377 cm
Inv. 1890 no. 8606

33. CENNI DI FRANCESCO
*Virgin and Child among eight
Saints and four Angels*
Late XIV century
Tempera on wood; 82x42 cm
Inv. 1890 no. 6119

34. GIOVANNI DEL BIONDO
Enthroned St. John the Evangelist
In the predella:
Ascension of St. John
c. 1380-1385
Tempera on wood; 335x112 cm
Inv. 1890 nos. 444, 446

35. GIOVANNI DEL BIONDO
*Presentation at the Temple among
St. John the Baptist and St. Benedict*
In the predella:
*Announcement to Zaccharia
Birth of the Baptist
Herod's banquet*
1364
Tempera on wood; 215x186 cm
Inv. 1890 no. 8462

13

JACOPO CAMBI
Coronation of the Virgin

This beautiful example of embroidery in *opus florentinum*, one of the most magnificent to come down to us, decorated the high altar of the Church of Santa Maria Novella in Florence. It was probably commissioned by Fra Jacopo of Andrea Aldobrandini, who was given other commissions for furnishings for the Dominican Monastery. The main scene with the *Coronation of the Virgin* is flanked by seven figures on each side, delimited to the right by the patriarch Abraham and to the left by king David. On the upper border are eleven stories from the life of Maria. In the lower center are the signature and the date: "IACOBUS CAMBI DE FLORENTIA ME FECIT MCCCXXXVI". Decorations of this type were highly appreciated and widely diffused in the Fourteenth century, especially in France and Spain, where another altar-facing embroidered by Geri di Lapo is still to be found in the Cathedral of Manresa in Catalonia. As compared to the latter, Jacopo Cambi's work is more elegant in the variety and fantasy of the stitches and in the Gothic style of the drawing. For the "ornate" naturalism of the figures and for some of the facial types (St. Peter and St. Paul), the most authoritative critics have linked this work to the refined culture of the Master of Figline.

17

ROSSELLO DI JACOPO FRANCHI
Coronation of the Virgin
with Angels and Saints

This grand and highly decorated polyptych
(1420) is the work of Rossello di Jacopo Franchi,
an artist who trained in the late Gothic period
and continued to paint his sweet and rather
mannered figures until the end of his life (1456),
long after the advent in Florence of Masaccio
and the rise of the early Renaissance.

20

GIOVANNI DAL PONTE
Coronation of the Virgin
with four musical Angels and Saints

Giovanni di Marco, known as Giovanni dal Ponte, received his nickname from the fact that he came from the florentine Parish of Santo Stefano al Ponte. He was an artist of great skill, clearly able to assimilate into his original artistic language the cultural influences emanating from the broad panorama of Florentine art in the early Fifteenth century. The artist was first attracted by Spinello Aretino, then by the Gothic International style introduced to Florence in those years by Lorenzo Monaco and Gherardo Starnina. In the third decade of the century (c. 1420-1430), to which this polyptych is dated, he freely adopted the Renaissance innovations introduced by Masolino, Beato Angelico and Masaccio, conferring greater composure on the figures but without abandoning his propensity to impetuous rhythms in the drawing as well as in the drapery of the figures.

23

SPINELLO ARETINO
St. Stephen

The saint is depicted holding in his right hand the banner of the Wool Guild, which was quite a powerful corporation in Florence and the same motif is repeated on the sides of the predella. This little tabernacle (c. 1400-1405) demonstrates the preciosity of Spinello's later style, and to a greater extent, the small *Crucifixion* in the cusp panel, where the drapery of the crouching figures flows with inimitable elegance.

24

NICCOLÒ DI PIETRO GERINI
Christ as the Man of Sorrows with the symbols of Passion

This panel (c. 1404-1408) is a typical example of the work of the Orcagna-trained painter Niccolò di Pietro Gerini and comes from the Disciplinary Company of the Pellegrino in Santa Maria Novella in Florence.

The brethren of the Company are depicted on the cusp kneeling in the foreground before Christ dressed as a pilgrim, and on the predella in the act of burying one of the members of their Company.

All the brethren wear white cloaks and their heads are covered by hoods, in order not to be recognised while carrying out works of charity. At the centre Christ rises from the tomb, showing the wounds in his hands and side, before the cross, on which are hung the symbols of Passion: nails, whips, the spear and the sponge.

28 MARIOTTO DI NARDO
Enthroned Virgin with Saints

This polyptych (c. 1390-1395), commissioned by the Corsini family for Church of St. Gaggio, records the mature phase of Mariotto di Nardo's work. It was an active artist in Florence between the Fourteenth and Fifteenth centuries, also for commissions of a certain importance. His success was probably due to the Orcagnesque elements in his style, the excessive hardness of which was diluted with warmer colouring and more charming decorative elements. The work by Mariotto reached us complete with all its elements, i.e. the predella showing *Scenes from the Life of the Virgin* and the large cuspidate panels with *Annunciation* and *Crucifixion*, and thus provides us with an idea of how ornate the altars of the most important Medieval churches must have been.

30

SPINELLO ARETINO
Enthroned Virgin and Child and four Angels with St. Paul, St. John the Baptist, St. Andrew and St. Matthew Evangelist

This altarpiece, which comes from the Church of Sant'Andrea a Lucca, is signed and dated 1391 on the step in the central panel. Spinello Aretino was first trained in the vigorous artistic atmosphere of Arezzo but later worked all over Tuscany – in addition to Arezzo and Lucca, Florence, where he worked for the Opera del Duomo in 1387; Pisa, where he frescoed the *Stories of Saints Efisio and Potito* in the Camposanto; Siena, where he worked in the Cathedral in 1405 and in the Sala di Balìa in Palazzo Pubblico in 1408. The Accademia Gallery possesses another work commissioned of Spinello, Niccolò Gerini and Lorenzo di Niccolò in 1399: the polyptych of the *Coronation of the Virgin and Saints* painted for the high altar of the Church of Santa Felicita in Florence (Inv. 1890 no. 8468). On a basic scheme that is still Giottesque, Spinello grafts episodes and details imbued with Gothic elegance in a style distinguished for its lively narration and vivid sense of decoration.

32

GIOVANNI DEL BIONDO
Annunciation

This large and complex polyptych (c. 1380) was situated on the altar of the Cavalcanti Chapel in Santa Maria Novella in Florence.
It came to us in excellent condition, complete with almost all its accessorie, and constitutes an example of the high technical quality of the work of Fourteenth century Florentine studios.

Lorenzo Monaco Room

The works

1. AGNOLO GADDI
The Virgin "del latte"
among St. John the Baptist,
St. Anthony abbot, St. Catherine,
and St. Mary Magdalene
c. 1380
Tempera on wood
92x54 cm
Inv. 1890 no. 8577

2. MASTER
OF SANTA VERDIANA
(TOMMASO DEL MAZZA)
Virgin of Humility
c. 1370-1400
Tempera on wood
87x49 cm
Inv. 1890 no. 3156

3. LORENZO MONACO
St. Caius Pope
St. Catherine of Alexandria
In the cuspid:
Our Lady of the Annunciation
and *Announcing Angel*
1395-1400
Tempera on wood
218x51 cm (each)
Inv. 1890 nos. 8604, 8605

4. LORENZO MONACO
St. Paul
St. Peter
St. John the Baptist
St. Moses
c. 1395-1400
Tempera on wood
100x40 cm (each)
Inv. 1890 nos. 8709, 8708,
8705, 8704

5. LORENZO MONACO
The Virgin "del latte"
with Saints and Angels
In the doors:
MASTER
OF THE SHERMAN PREDELLA
Annunciation, Crucifixion
with mourners and Saints
c. 1390, 1425-1430
Tempera on wood
148x140 cm
Inv. 1890 no. 3227

6. RUSSIAN SCHOOL
84 Icons
XVII-XVIII centuries
Tempera/oil on wood

7. BARTOLOMEO DI FRUOSINO
Painted Cross
1411
Tempera on wood
280x190 cm
Inv. 1890 no. 3147

8. LORENZO MONACO
Painted Cross
c. 1400-1410
Tempera on wood
220x190 cm
Inv. 1890 no. 3153

9. LORENZO MONACO
Annunciation among St.Catherine
of Alexandria, St. Anthony,
St. Proculous and St. Francis
c. 1418
Tempera on wood
210x229 cm
Inv. 1890 no. 8458

10. LORENZO MONACO
Sorrowing Virgin
Christ Crucified and Angels
St. John the Evangelist
c. 1400-1413
Tempera on wood
48x43 cm (side panels)
59x35 cm (central panel)
Inv. 1890 nos. 2169, 2140, 2141

11. LORENZO MONACO
Enthroned Virgin and Child
among two Angels and St.
Bartholomew, St. John the Baptist,
St. Thaddeus and St. Benedict
In the cuspids:
Announcing Angel,
Benediction of Christ
and *Our Lady of the Annunciation*
In the pinnacles:
Two Prophets
1410
Tempera on wood; 274x259 cm
Inv. 1890 no. 468

12. LORENZO MONACO
Virgin and Child with Saints
1408
Tempera on wood
89x49 cm
Inv. 1890 no. 470

13. LORENZO MONACO
Christ as the Man of Sorrows
with the symbols of Passion
1404
Tempera on wood
268x170 cm
Inv. 1890 no. 467

14. LORENZO MONACO
Oration in the Garden
c. 1395-1400
Tempera on wood
222x49 cm
Inv. 1890 no. 438

15. ANONYMOUS FLORENTINE
Coronation of the Virgin
with Saints
In the cuspid:
Benediction of the Eternal Father
c. 1390-1399
Tempera on wood
111x53 cm
Inv. 1890 no. 8579

16. AGNOLO GADDI
Virgin of Humility
with six Angels
c. 1390-1396
Tempera on wood
118x58 cm
Inv. 1890 no. 461

THE COLLECTION OF RUSSIAN ICONS

The Collection of Russian Icons, put together by the Grand Dukes of Lorraine, is displayed in the niches of the right-hand wall. The quality of these pieces is rather discontinuous and only rarely of exceptional calibre; therefore it might be said that the group as a whole is more significant for research and knowledge of the Lorraine passion for collecting rather than for the history of Russian art.

6

RUSSIAN SCHOOL
St. Catherine

Catherine is portrayed with her usual attributes, i.e. the palm of martyrdom in her right hand and the hooked wheel on which she was tortured before her head was cut off. The image (18th century) is decorated with a crown and a fine silver-gilt frame.

SCA·CATHARINE SCS·ANTONIUS AVE·GRATIA·PLENA ECCE·ANCILLA·DOMINI SCS·PROCULUS SCS·FRANCISC

9

LORENZO MONACO
Annunciation and Saints

Painted for the Florentine Badia, this Annunciation represents the peak of Lorenzo Monaco's work; in the period in which Masaccio, initiator of the artistic Renaissance, was beginning to work, the Medieval world is brought to life with brilliant success in this work (c. 1418).

117

11

LORENZO MONACO
Enthroned Virgin and Child

This polyptych (1410) formerly decorated the Church of San Bartolomeo in Montoliveto near Florence and confirms Lorenzo Monaco's ability with chromatic and decorative effects, even in works of larger dimensions.

Having now fully mastered his expressive medium, the great master emphasises here the outlines of the figures with impeccable fluidity and harmony while the chromatic range seems infused with the purest light.

It must be remembered that Lorenzo Monaco was also an illuminator and his pen decorated with gold and bright colours many of the manuscripts made in the Monastery of Santa Maria degli Angioli in Florence, where he lived as a Camaldolensian monk.

14

LORENZO MONACO
The oration in the Garden

This is one of the oldest panels by Lorenzo Monaco and was painted (c. 1395-1400) for the Florentine Monastery of Santa Maria degli Angioli, where the artist lived. His deep knowledge of Giotto's painting, who must have been directly known to him, is evident from the style, learned in the Orcagna studio.

However, at the same time the fluid and extended flowing of the drapery places his work within the modern taste for International Gothicism.

International Gothic Room

The works

1. **MASTER OF THE STRAUS MADONNA**
   Christ as the Man of Sorrows with the symbols of the Passion
   c. 1400-1405
   Tempera on wood
   123x240 cm
   Dep. Inv. no. 14

2. **MASTER OF SANT'IVO**
   Virgin with Child and Saints
   c. 1400-1415
   Tempera on wood
   77x42 cm
   Inv. 1890 no. 8614

3. **MASTER OF 1416**
   Virgin with Child and Saints
   In the cuspid: *Ethernal Father*
   1416
   Tempera on wood
   231x115 cm
   Inv. 1890 no. 4635

4. **MASTER OF SANT'IVO**
   Virgin and Child with four Saints
   c. 1390-1410
   Tempera on wood
   57x43 cm
   Inv. 1890 no. 3151

5. **MASTER OF BORGO ALLA COLLINA**
   Enthroned Virgin and Child with Saints
   In the cuspid:
   The Crucifix between St. Sebastian and St. Julian
   c. 1420
   Tempera on wood
   178x80 cm
   Inv. 1890 no. 478

6. **MASTER OF THE SHERMAN PREDELLA**
   Crucifixion
   c. 1415-1430
   Tempera on wood
   45x80 cm
   Inv. 1890 no. 4654

7. **BICCI DI LORENZO**
   St. Lawrence
   In the predella:
   Scenes from the life of St. Lawrence
   c. 1428
   Tempera on wood
   236x84 cm
   Inv. 1890 no. 471

8. **BICCI DI LORENZO**
   Mystic marriage of St. Catherine
   c. 1423-1425
   Tempera on wood
   125x59 cm
   Inv. 1890 no. 8611

9. **ROSSELLO DI JACOPO FRANCHI**
   Virgin and Child with Saints
   In the cuspids:
   Crucifixion with Saints
   First half of XV century
   Tempera on wood
   238x190 cm
   Inv. 1890 no. 475

10. **MASTER OF BORGO ALLA COLLINA**
    Virgin and Child with four Saints
    c. 1430
    Tempera on wood
    127x65 cm
    Inv. 1890 no. 3159

11. **GIOVANNI TOSCANI**
    Virgin and Child among Saints and musical Angels
    1423-1424
    Tempera on wood
    148x102 cm
    Inv. 1890 no. 5919

12. **GIOVANNI TOSCANI**
    In the cuspid: *Crucifixion*
    In the predella:
    Stigmata of St. Francis and
    Miracle of St. Nicolas of Bari
    c. 1423-1424
    Tempera on wood
    125x46 cm; 33x62 cm
    Inv. 1890 nos. 6089, 3333

13. **GIOVANNI TOSCANI**
    Incredulity of St. Thomas
    c. 1420
    Tempera on wood
    240x112 cm
    Inv. 1890 no. 457

14. **FLORENTINE PAINTER**
    St. Peter and St. Eustace
    (On the back: *The prophet Jeremiah and Angel's head*),
    St. Jerome and Saint with book
    (On the back: *Angel with thurible*),
    St. Nicolas and St. Peter
    (On the back: *The Prophet Isaiah [?] and Angel's head*),
    St. Reparata (or Dorothy) and St. James
    (On the back: *Angel with thurible*)
    c. 1410
    Tempera on wood
    25x65 cm (each)
    Inv. 1890 nos. 6116, 6117, 6118, 6132

15. **MASTER OF THE STRAUS MADONNA**
    Annunciation
    c. 1395-1405
    Tempera on wood
    190x200 cm
    Inv. 1890 no. 3146

16. **MASTER OF THE STRAUS MADONNA**
    St. Francis
    St. Catherine of Alexandria
    c. 1400-1410
    Tempera on wood
    56x23 cm (each)
    Inv. 1890 nos. 476, 477

17. **GHERARDO STARNINA**
    Virgin and Child with St. John the Baptist, St. Nicolas and Angels
    c. 1407-1410
    Tempera on wood
    96x51 cm
    Inv. 1890 no. 441

7

BICCI DI LORENZO
St. Lawrence

This panel comes from the Laical Company devoted to St. Peter at the Church of San Pietro a Monticelli.

The Saint is shown standing on the symbol of his martyrdom, the grille, while in his left hand he holds the palm and in the right a red banner with a gold star, perhaps the insignia of the Company who commissioned the work.

In the predella, in the right-hand scene, St. Lawrence is depicted freeing souls from Purgatory, according to the legend which claims that as he died on Good Friday, he was permitted every Friday to repeat Christ's descent to the Underworld. The scene on the left shows the martyrdom inflicted on him by his persecutors.

Bicci di Lorenzo painted this work in about 1428, in collaboration with Stefano d'Antonio with whom he "kept company" (or as we would say today "was in partnership") from 1426 to 1434.

12

GIOVANNI TOSCANI
Crucifixion (cuspid)
Stigmata of St. Francis and *Miracle
of St. Nicolas of Bari* (predella)

These two panels, dating from the beginning of the third decade of the Fifteenth century, formed part of the polyptych adorning the Ardinghelli Chapel in the Church of Santa Trinita at Florence. The painter was a Florentine artist, enrolled in the Compagnia di San Luca in 1424, known especially as a painter of chests (two of his chests are now in the Bargello Museum).

His earliest works, such the *Incredulity of St. Thomas* in the Accademia Gallery, reveal train-ing in contact with the Orcagna circle as well as the influence of Ghiberti's style, particularly in the rhythmic folds of the drapery. This element has led some scholars to identify the artist as Giovanni di Francesco, one of Ghiberti's assistants for the doors of the Baptistery. Within a span of ten years Giovanni Toscani shows in these two panels how he has assimilated the innovations of the International Gothic Style introduced to Florence by Gentile da Fabriano and Arcangelo di Cola.

15

MASTER
OF THE STRAUS MADONNA
Annunciation

This work came from the leper Hospital of Sant'Eusebio al Prato and is attributed to a painter who was active between the end of the Fourteenth century and the beginning of the Fifteenth. His identity is not known and he is usually known as the Master of the Straus Madonna from a *Virgin with Child* in the Straus Collection. This is a painter gifted with fine sensitivity to colour and who also pays attention to the volumetric structure of bodies and the perspective depth of the space.

17

GHERARDO STARNINA
Virgin and Child,
with Saints and Angels

Gherardo Starnina, a Florentine painter who also worked in Spain where he came into contact with the most advanced trends of International Gothicism, today tends to be identified by critics as the so-called Master of the Lively Child, an outstanding figure in early Fifteenth century painting in Florence. He was noted for his linear finesse and the decorative nature of his elegant forms, and is almost a profane *alter ego* of Lorenzo Monaco.

Index of names

Printed in May 2001
by Giunti Industrie Grafiche S.p.A.
Prato